TO SOUND LIKE YOURSELF

ESSAYS ON POETRY

BY

W. D. Snodgrass

AMERICAN READER SERIES, NO. 5

WILMETTE PUBLIC LIBRARY

BOA Editions, Ltd. ◉ Rochester, NY ◉ 2002

Copyright © 2002 by W. D. Snodgrass
All rights reserved
Manufactured in the United States of America

First Edition
02 03 04 05   7 6 5 4 3 2 1

Publications by BOA Editions, Ltd.—
a not-for-profit corporation under section 501 (c) (3)
of the United States Internal Revenue Code—
are made possible with the assistance of grants from
the Literature Program of the New York State Council on the Arts,
the Literature Program of the National Endowment for the Arts,
the Sonia Raiziss Giop Charitable Foundation,
the Lannan Foundation,
as well as from the Mary S. Mulligan Charitable Trust,
the County of Monroe, NY,
Ames-Amzalak Memorial Trust,
and The CIRE Foundation.

See page 244 for special individual acknowledgments.

Cover Design: Lisa Mauro
Cover Art: "W.D. and the Amigo," by DeLoss McGraw, courtesy of the artist
Interior Design and Typesetting: Richard Foerster
Manufacturing: McNaughton & Gunn, Lithographers
BOA Logo: Mirko

LIBRARY OF CONGRESS CATALOGING-IN-PUBLICATION DATA

Snodgrass, W. D. (William De Witt), 1926–
   To sound like yourself : essays on poetry / by W.D. Snodgrass.
      p. cm. — (American reader series ; no. 5)
   Includes index.
   ISBN 1-929918-18-6
   1. Snodgrass, W. D. (William De Witt), 1926---Aesthetics. 2. Whitman, Walt,
1819–1892--Criticism and interpretation. 3. Poetry. I. Title. II. American reader
series ; no. 5.

PS3537.N32 T6 2002
809.1—dc21

2002074593

BOA Editions, Ltd.
Steven Huff, Publisher
H. Allen Spencer, Chair
A. Poulin, Jr., President & Founder (1976–1996)
260 East Avenue, Rochester, NY 14604
www.boaeditions.org

11.09
Snodgrass,
W.

Man, sometimes it takes you a long time to sound like yourself.

—Miles Davis

For Kathy

without whom, not

CONTENTS

PULSE AND IMPULSE

I. Good Gray Poets and Great Horned Owls

My fix upon the owl as a household Lar and totem must have begun that night when my third wife and I were moving into an old farmhouse near Erieville, N.Y. On toward midnight we were still lugging in boxes and chairs when, startlingly close, a Great Horned Owl spoke, loud and imperious, from the woods that we had taken to be ours. A few days earlier, I had tromped those woods chanting in mock triumph, "Whose woods these are I think I know; whose woods these are I think I know . . ." It was now clear that ours would be, at best, a joint title.

The nest was perched in a huge beech tree near the woods' edge—until the leaves spread, we could see it from our kitchen window, though for some years we never saw the owls. In the colder months, we heard them night after night, going out to hunt about 11 o'clock, then coming back around 4 or 5. During their mating season—the dead cold of January and February—the male's voice grows superbly resonant. Though smaller and less aggressive, he speaks first; she answers about a fourth higher. Gradually, their calls sound closer together until they stretto, or overlap, in a sort of harmony. Soon my wife and I—who, only months before, had spent our nights prowling the belly dance joints of Detroit—nightly roamed the woods with a tape recorder. Sometimes, during the feasts we perpetrated upon friends from Syracuse University, George P. Elliott would stagger to our couch, asking to hear one of our owl tapes during the ten-minute nap he needed before confronting the next course. Those voices are indeed beautiful and calming—if they portend that you will soon eat, rather than be eaten!

For no apparent reason, though, in our sixth or seventh year there, the female owl began to let herself be seen, peering over the nest's edge until, if we came too close, she would dive down, soaring off through the woods. She looked roughly like a Saint Bernard with awnings. Later that year, in a sharp storm, her nest came down; for several weeks we foster-parented two balls of under-bed phnuff the size of hornets' nests. Centered in each ball were huge, yellowy eyes and a beak that clacked menacingly until you gave the adult owls' call; then the fuzzballs sighed and clucked contentedly, cuddling up to feed or sleep. After our local hawk and owl expert discovered the parent birds still lurking nearby, we built a huge new nest—a plastic laundry basket filled with branches, sticks and twigs—and hauled it up into a hedgerow tree where we could watch from a back window as the real parents tended their young. Every morning the mother owl was up there doing her nestwork: tearing up large fish and groundhogs, rearranging twigs, grooming her babies. And, I confess, we climbed a ladder most afternoons to give them an extra feeding.

The following year, our bird expert, the local postmaster, turned up an orphan. In the post office lobby one morning, he'd found a cardboard box containing a baby Great Horned Owl. Unsure which nest it had fallen from, he offered to let us raise it, warning that we'd not only have to feed it, but also teach it to fly and hunt. For months, I cruised the back roads for roadkills—small animals or birds that could be hauled home, chopped up with an axe, frozen and later fed to my ravenous phnuffball. Some of those carcasses were not of the sweetest; racing home ahead of the stench from my trunk, I gleefully imagined the confrontation if some state trooper should stop me and demand to search my car!

When the owl became large enough to fly—we had named her Bubolina Bufnitsa—we kept her in a nearby cabin where she could strengthen her wings while we taught her to hunt. Several times a day I ventured in to drag food in front of her on a string; later I made her snatch it on the wing. I'm not sure I ever did anything quite so strange.

All this may suggest something of *why* I should write about owls, but nothing of *how*—that had to do with studies in rhythm and prosody. During that same period I'd been experimenting with a technique I'd come across in Walt Whitman, our first and greatest free verse poet. Often, in a poem's first line—or first half-line—he would state a rhythm which he could then develop much like the musical theme for a set of variations. In his Civil War book, *Drum-Taps*, for instance, an overly famous poem begins with half-line motifs, each with three heavy beats:

/   /   /   /   / ˘ /
Beat! beat! drums — blow! bugles! blow!

Elsewhere, however, he used this three-beat motif subtly and flexibly in one of his best short poems, "Cavalry Crossing a Ford":

A line in long array   where they wind betwixt green islands.

The pattern appears again in the very next poem, the equally fine "Bivouac on a Mountain Side":

I see before me now   a travelling army halting

Having twice stated its theme, each poem then sets out to build upon that—lengthening, altering, sophisticating, stress-loading. The resulting structure of rhythms IS that poem's music, closely involved with its structures of rhetoric and imagery.

The most striking example, however, from the book *Sea-Drift*, takes a rhythm not of three but of two beats:

/ ˘ ˘ / ˘   / ˘ ˘ / ˘
Out of the cradle   endlessly rocking,

a rhythm which suggests not only the motions of a cradle or of the sea but of the most deep-set rhythms of our lives. As I will comment on these poems elsewhere in this book, I shall forgo discussing their fuller rhythmic structure here. I may note, however, that some years before I had worked as a percussionist on a performance of this poem with drums and had found the underlying rhythm of this passage to be either a 7/8:

$\frac{7}{8}$ | ♪ ♪ ♪ ♩ ♩| ♪ ♪ ♪ ♩ ♩ |
Out of the cradle, endlessly rocking

or, perhaps, a syncopation between constant measures which, at will, vary 3 notes with 2:

$\frac{3}{8}$ | ♪ ♪ ♪ | ♩ ♩ | ♪ ♪ ♪ ♪ | ♩ ♩ |

Out of the cradle, endlessly rocking

I have often encountered such rhythms in the belly dance joints of Detroit and in various musics produced outside of eighteenth and nineteenth century Europe. It is unlikely that Whitman, fond of folk songs, of marches and Italian opera, would have encountered music of this sort. He'd have been likely to hear such rhythms only internally—uneven or irregular rhythms being more typical of the body's sounds than are the insistent regularities of Western classical and popular music. Given this poem's subject matter and its underlying motifs of the "mother" sea, I associate this rhythm with the mother's heartbeat and those other bodily rhythms which are constantly transmitted into the amniotic fluid of the womb. (This recalls a folk remedy: to soothe a puppy newly taken from its mother, you wrap a towel around a big wind-up clock and put that in its bed. Admittedly, we don't do that for our children; we *do* rock them, sing, speak and chant rhythmically to comfort them.)

In any case, despite Whitman's abandonment of traditional English metrics, and unlike so much later free verse, the poem has a strong rhythmic impulse. During the opening verse paragraph, that rhythm and its variants nearly override the message content:

> Out of the cradle, endlessly rocking,
> Out of the mockingbird's throat, the musical shuttle,
> Out of the Ninth-month midnight,
> Over the sterile sands and the fields beyond, where the
>   child leaving his bed wander'd alone, bareheaded,
>   barefoot,
> Down from the shower'd halo,
> Up from the mystic play of shadows twining and twisting
>   as if they were alive,
> Out from the patches of briers and blackberries,
> From the memories of the bird that chanted to me,
> From your memories sad brother, from the fitful risings
>   and fallings I heard,

From under that yellow half-moon, late-risen and swollen
    as if with tears,
From those beginning notes of yearning and love there in
    the mist,
From the thousand responses of my heart never to cease,
From the myriad thence-arous'd words,
From the word stronger and more delicious than any,
From such as now they start the scene revisiting,
As a flock, twittering, rising, or overhead passing,
Borne hither, ere all eludes me, hurriedly,
A man, yet by these tears a little boy again,
Throwing myself on the sand, confronting the waves,
I, chanter of pains and joys, uniter of here and hereafter,
Taking all hints to use them, but swiftly leaping beyond
    them,
A reminiscence sing.

Whitman's process of composition here, as evidenced by his revisions, was just the opposite of what you'd expect. Rather than pick a theme, then develop variations from that, he worked back through the variations toward the theme, only discovering that (the poem's present first line) very late in the process. The poem was first printed in the third (1860) edition of *Leaves of Grass*, beginning

    Out of the rock'd cradle,

a line without strong rhythmic impulse and with little relation to the poem's later musics. The present opening first surfaces in a handwritten revision for the1867 edition; although several echoes of it are heard in succeeding lines, Whitman rejected it at that time in favor of the first line from 1860. Only in 1871 did the theme (with the new first line and title) emerge into print.

As one might expect in so long and complex a composition, other techniques and devices take over after this first section and control the body of the poem. These have been fully explored by others and need no comment here. However, just when a reader has almost forgotten that rhythm, Whitman fetches it back for his coda:

> . . . [I] fuse the song of my dusky demon and brother,
> That he sang to me in the moonlight on Paumanok's gray
>   beach,
> With the thousand responsive songs at random,
> My own songs awaked from that hour,
> And with them the word up from the waves,
> The word of the sweetest song and of all songs,
> (Or like some old crone, rocking the cradle, swathed in
>   sweet garments, bending aside,)
> The sea whispered me.

The parenthetical resurgence of that primal rhythm — a stroke of sheerest genius — appeared only in the seventh edition of 1881, just before the "Deathbed" version!

For my own first venture along such lines, a poem based on Vincent Van Gogh's painting, "The Starry Night," I decided not to take a rhythm as my theme, fearing this might seem too directly derivative. I took instead the pattern of vowels in the painter's last reported words, "Zóó heen kan gaan," and formed my poem's major sections from variations on that sound pattern. In the first section, for instance, each of those vowels appears twice before we move on to the next:

> Row on row, the gray frame cottages, small

and so on through the poem. Influenced by Vincent D'Indy's *Ishtar Variations*—and perhaps by my recognition of Whitman's progression from variation to theme—I decided to introduce my theme, the painter's last words, only in the poem's last line. Thus I hoped to give the whole a sort of musical unity together with a sense of musical closure—something like what we derive, elsewhere, from rhyme.

Encouraged by work on this poem, I decided after all to try a rhythmic theme, though I wanted one sharply different from any of Whitman's. By this time, I had become deeply involved with owl sounds—had in fact been making owl calls. Once I had released my baby owl, now a "teenager," I was astonished at my sense of loss. I went out almost every evening and called; nothing answered. Nights became emptier than I had thought possible. Then one evening, after ten days or so, a tremendous impact on our tin roof announced her return, hopping mad and shrieking for some of the plastic-wrapped woodchuck dainties I had packed into our deep freeze. For the next several months, every evening I went up to our woods and called — five notes:

HOO, hoo HOO, HOO, HOO.

Answering with the baby's hunger screech, she'd come sailing in to me, immense and beautiful, on wings at least 5' in span. This lasted several months; then, one night, when I gave the adult call, she answered from one side; simultaneously, from the valley below, a deeper and darker call resounded. An adult male had arrived; I did not see her again for eight years. But since I imagined her to be out hunting with that Sarastro-toned male, all seemed well and good.

I now intended, though, a more intimate involvement with those owl calls. Earlier, I had written a poem, "Regraduating the Lute," comparing the development of a musical instrument's sound to the maturation of one's own voice, one's own music, in a love relationship. I now imagined—mistakenly, it turned out—that the voices of our owls as they went out to hunt together, their calls resounding back and forth across a cold and dark expanse, might correspond to the relation between my wife and myself.

Feeling that I had written too often about love's troubles, and wanting to celebrate what seemed a fulfilled and fulfilling relationship, I took the rhythm of those calls

HOO, hoo HOO, HOO, HOO

as the basis of a poem for my wife. The first line reproduces that four-beat rhythm:

Wait, the Great Horned Owls,

while the second adds several light syllables:

17

Calling from the woods' edge, listen.

The third drops back to the basic pattern:

There: the dark male, low

but the fourth adds even more light syllables:

And booming, tremoring the whole valley.

And so on throughout the poem:

OWLS

Wait; the great horned owls
Calling from the wood's edge; listen.
There: the dark male, low
And booming, tremoring the whole valley.
There: the female, resolving, answering
High and clear, restoring silence.
The chilly woods draw in
Their breath, slow, waiting, and now both
Sound out together, close to harmony.

These are the year's worst nights.
Ice glazed on the top boughs.
Old snow deep on the ground,
Snow in the red-tailed hawks'
Nests they take for their own.
Nothing crosses the crusted ground.
No squirrels, no rabbits, the mice gone,
No crow has young yet they can steal.
These nights the iron air clangs
Like the gates of a cell block, blank
And black as the inside of your chest.

Now, the great owls take
The air, the male's calls take
Depth on and resonance, they take
A rough nest, take their mate
And, opening out long wings, take
Flight, unguided and apart, to caliper
The blind synapse their voices cross
Over the dead white fields,
The dead black woods, where they take
Soundings on nothing fast, take
Soundings on each other, each alone.

When such a music works, it seems not merely to restrain or limit the poem's energies; it comes to be identified with that energy itself, an energy which can only be realized as it is controlled and channeled.

I'm not suggesting that's true of this poem — you never know whether your own work works. Or your own love relationships. That marriage, in time, broke up and that house stood vacant for several years. Yet, one autumn, eight years after my owl had heard that new call and flown off with her mate, I came to live there once again, though with my fourth wife. One evening she burst into the living room, stammering with excitement, "An owl, an owl, outside, an owl!" There, perched in the big oak on our lawn, only a few feet away, sat a burly Great Horned Owl. When I gave the adult's call, it answered with the baby's screech. It *was* the same owl, the true Bubolina Bufnitsa—huge, healthy and still responsive to her early imprinting. She even accepted my new wife as a sort of stepmother—who nearly got frost-bitten standing out in the October chill, talking with her night after night until the time arrived for our migration to Mexico, leaving our step-bird to pick over the local small game and raise her brood of phnuffballs. Which gave me, besides, the satisfaction of thinking that she had proved notably more faithful—or was it only hungrier? (or is that really the same?)—than quite a few friends and lovers.

II. APPLE TREES AND BELLY DANCERS

Among American poets, a favorite indoor sport is to set a revered poem to an outrageous popular melody—a tune whose rhythm fits the text, but whose mood and movement ruthlessly desecrate it. At a party, someone may regale you with Wordsworth's "She Dwelt Among the Untrodden Ways" sung to the tune of "Yankee Doodle." You'll hear Blake's "Tyger" sung to "Tea for Two"; Donne's "Valediction Forbidding Mourning" to "The Syncopated Clock" or *The Iliad* in Greek to "Stars and Stripes Forever." Competitions may break out for "Stopping by Woods on a Snowy Evening"— a Gregorian Kyrie vs. "Ein Feste Burg"; "O Tannenbaum" vs. "The William Tell Overture." The winner will always be "Hernando's Hideaway." We are like lovers who dare express ourselves only in mocking raillery lest we be obliterated by our own adoration.

Just the reverse can happen when writing: the rhythm of a piece of music may take a decisive hand in shaping a poem— perhaps a work of greater consequence than the music that helped form it. In his essay, "The Music of Poetry," T. S. Eliot wrote:

> I know that a poem, or a passage of a poem, may tend to realize itself first as a particular rhythm before it reaches expression in words, and that this rhythm may bring to birth the idea and the image; and I do not believe that this is an experience peculiar to myself.

William Butler Yeats went further, saying that poems often first came to him not only as a rhythm, but as a phrase of melody. My own special party routine is to sing the first stanza of "The Love Song of J. Alfred Prufrock" to the tune of "Ain't Misbehavin'." They fit so astonishingly well that for years I dreamed I could set the critical world on its tin ear by demonstrating Eliot's remark from his own practice and using an example which might have shocked him most of all. Still, in the poem, the real motive behind J. Alfred's endless rationalizations *is* to talk himself out of "misbehavin'"— out of paying a "visit" to ask a lady "an overwhelming question."

Moreover, Eliot had come from St. Louis, the same city where "Fats" Waller had played piano and sung.

Alas, the song was published three years *after* the poem. No doubt Waller would have been playing it for some time before its publication and Eliot could have heard it then, yet it seems improbable that he'd have frequented the places where Waller played. So I set out on a lesser conquest: to demonstrate Eliot's theory from my own experience. He might have thought my example—involving a stand of wormy old apple trees, various belly dancers, transvestites, strippers and a cheap Broadway show tune—even less savory. Couldn't I at least have chosen something from *The St. Matthew Passion*?

Some time after I'd worked out my variations on the owl's call which I've already described, I decided to try those methods for a longer poem. I'd been having a gawdawful time trying to write about the overgrown apple orchard on our place in upstate New York. I'd tried several meters, then a long-lined free verse; nothing worked. I now picked a theme—at random, I thought—which I hoped would be sufficiently different from any I'd tried before:

‿ / ‿ ‿ / /

As Whitman often did, I stated that theme twice in my first line:

Like battered old millhands, they stand in the orchard—

Once I'd struck on this rhythm, the poem came with surprising speed:

OLD APPLE TREES

Like battered old millhands, they stand in the orchard—
Like drunk legionnaires, heaving themselves up,
Lurching to attention. Not one of them wobbles
The same way as another. Uniforms won't fit them—
All those cramps, humps, bulges. Here, a limb's gone;

21

There, rain and corruption have eaten the whole core.
They've all grown too tall, too thick, or too something.
Like men bent too long over desks, engines, benches,
Or bent under mailsacks, under loss.
They've seen too much history and bad weather, grown
Around rocks, into high winds, diseases, grown
Too long to be wilful, too long to be changed.

Oh, I could replant, bulldoze the lot,
Get nursery stock, all the latest ornamentals,
Make the whole place look like a suburb,
Each limb sleek as a teenybopper's—pink
To the very crotch—each trunk smoothed, ideal
As the fantasy life of an adman.
We might just own the Arboreal Muscle Beach:
Each tree disguised as its neighbor. Or each disguised
As if not its neighbor—each doing its own thing
Like executives' children.

                              At least I could prune,
At least I should trim the dead wood; fill holes
Where rain collects and decay starts. Well, I should;
I should. There's a red squirrel nests here someplace.
I live in the hope of hearing one saw-whet owl.
Then, too, they're right about Spring. Bees hum
Through these branches like lascivious intentions. The
Petals drift down, sift across the ground; this air's so rich
No man should come here except on a working pass;
No man should leave here without going to confession.
All Fall, apples nearly crack the boughs;
They hang here red as candles in the
White oncoming snow.

Tonight we'll drive down to the bad part of town
To the New Hungarian Bar or the Klub Polski,
To the Old Hellas where we'll eat the new spring lamb;
                              [no stanza break]

Drink good *mavrodaphne*, say, at the Laikon Bar,
Send drinks to the dancers, those meatcutters and laborers
Who move in their native dances, the archaic forms.
Maybe we'll still find our old crone selling chestnuts,
Whose toothless gums can spit out fifteen languages,
Who turns, there, late at night, in the center of the floor,
Her ancient dry hips wheeling their slow, slow *tsamikos*;
We'll stomp under the tables, whistle, we'll all hiss
Till even the belly dancer leaves, disgraced.

We'll drive back, lushed and vacant, in the first dawn;
Out of the light gray mists may rise our flowering
Orchard, the rough trunks holding their formations
Like elders of Colonus, the old men of Thebes
Tossing their white hair, almost whispering,

> Soon, each one of us will be taken
> By dark powers under this ground
> That drove us here, that warped us.
> Not one of us got it his own way.
> Nothing like any one of us
> Will be seen again, forever.
> Each of us held some noble shape in mind.
> It seemed better that we kept alive.

Let me go back now and scan the first eight half-lines to clarify
their rhythmic derivation from the theme I'd chosen:

⏑   / ⏑ \ / /
Like battered old millhands

⏑   / ⏑ ⏑ / ⏑
they stand in the orchard —

⏑   / \ ⏑ /
Like drunk legionnaires,

/ ˘ ˘ / /
heaving themselves up,

/ ˘ ˘ ˘ / ˘
Lurching to attention.

\ / ˘ ˘ / ˘
Not one of them wobbles

˘ / / ˘ ˘ / ˘
The same way as another.

/ ˘ ˘ \ / /
Uniforms won't fit them—

Though variants become more drastic later, the first three stanzas run easily enough in comparing my trees to men bent and misshapen by hard lives. No doubt I was thinking of my upstate New York neighbors, the farmers, postmasters or grocery clerks whom I saw in Fourth of July parades. Somehow they'd cramped their outsized stomachs, bent backs and uneven legs into their old uniforms; down the street they wobbled, some in time with a band ahead, others with a band behind, some solemn as church, others grinning broadly, all laced with liquid high spirits.

One Fourth of July, I'd been privileged to watch the Ladies' Auxiliary of Scottsville, N.Y. They, in contrast to the male veterans, were trim and soldierly: smartly uniformed in white, precise in line and step, they executed intricate patterns, crisscrossing at angles, their lines doubling back on themselves. Purportedly leading those formations, the dead-drunk mayor of the village shambled along, unable to walk a straight line, constantly surrounded and gobbled up by the interweaving lines of the ladies' elegant maneuvers.

Looking at my poem now, I suppose it contrasts my orchard with that of a rich lawyer who lives down the road. His apple trees look like orchards *should*: each about 12 or 15 feet tall, lined up front to back, side to side, diagonal against diagonal. If I had any decent instincts, my poem would probably compare my neighbor's trees to the Ladies' Auxiliary and my trees to the drunken mayor. I'm afraid it doesn't. More likely, I feel some reproach from my neighbor's tidy, productive orchard and am trying, here, to defend my trees by demeaning his.

If you cut off a tree's leader, the highest upreaching branch, it sends up a substitute leader. It has, seemingly, an ideal of form, keeps a shape in mind which it tries to achieve. Having had all the advantages, my neighbor's trees all look alike. Sheltered from exterior events or forces and all subject to the same inherent drive toward form, his trees come to look almost mass-produced, turned out of molds.

Each of my trees looks like none you've ever seen before. Grown before the days of sprays and tree spikes, they reflect the differences in soils, in seasons. You couldn't grow such trees to-day—once insecticides have been introduced, they become a neces-sity. Now, any tree planted in the area and not sprayed every two weeks dies in three. So my trees, however misshapen, have a certain heroic cast for me. One I *did* cut down (it had lost a main branch and rot would soon hollow it out) had a butt log 20 feet long and 23 inches in diameter! Our local sawyer had never seen anything like it; *you* never saw anything like the two-inch apple boards it gave me.

True, my trees don't give me apples; I can afford to sneer at my neighbor's trees only because he lets me pick them. My trees, though, give me red squirrels, grouse, wild turkeys, white-tailed deer. What could I imagine inhabiting *his* orchard but one of those numbered and life-sentenced chickens that never sees dirt, never eats bugs, yet fills our supermarkets with identical boxes of per-fectly tasteless, perfectly sterile eggs?

By the time I've reached the phrase "each disguised as if not its neighbor," it's clear, even to me, that I'm scarcely talking about trees, or even about my neighbor. More likely, I'm biting still other hands that feed me—talking about some of my less admirable students who, I fear, share certain qualities with those supermarket chickens. Unquestionably, I am talking about the American middle class and its failure to turn freedom and prosperity into creative

25

individuality—a failure disguised alternately by gaudy self-displays of costume and manner, then by blameful demands for still more freedom, still more unfair advantages.

I see just such qualities, too, in the poems some of my students, like some of their elders, write—poems which have had *no* outside pressures and seem thus to have lost any shaping by events. My trees may be warped and twisted; I prefer them to scrub brush or kudzu. If I seem to be preaching, it is to an audience of one. I am of the American middle class and its problems have obsessed my life and work: freedom from outside pressures can leave you at the scant mercies of your inner drives. So I must at least admire a less protected, admittedly trouble-filled, possibly dangerous fertility and growth—a life created in that (often enough, deadly) struggle between the internal drive toward a desired form and the unpredictable events and stresses of the world. That, I think, is the essential argument of my first three stanzas.

Something strange, though, happens at the beginning of the fourth stanza, "Tonight we'll drive down to the bad part of town": the poem changes locales. There may be places in America where you could drive easily from the opening's rural scene into an urban setting. But, assuredly, no belly dance joint lies within driving distance of Erieville, N.Y., where that orchard stands. The poem's clubs and bars, their names slightly changed, were places my former wife and I had frequented in Detroit almost ten years before: the Arabic, Armenian, and, especially, the Greek belly dance joints where local artists and intellectuals hung out nightly. Those places were a wonderful respite from American middle-class life. Many we'd found there were ordinary laborers, not unlike the upstate farm workers of my earlier stanzas; many were recent immigrants like those who worked the steel mills of my childhood near Pittsburgh, Pennsylvania. No doubt, the "millhands" of the poem's first line pointed toward this linkage.

Still, it was odd to have hauled that Detroit scene into my apparently pastoral poem. Even as I did it, one side of my mind was panicking: "It won't work! That's ten years ago! Three hundred miles! The landscapes won't blend!" But somehow, another part, wanting that belly dance scene, kept saying, "I dare you!"

I was relieved, when I came to the fifth stanza, to be able to link the two scenes by returning to the farm and seeing our old trees there as a different kind of Greek dance— something in one of the Greek tragedies. I had long suspected that the music and dancing in those dramas should be far wilder than the solemn chants and stately movements most readers, like most stage productions, then assumed. Besides, in mentioning the old men of Thebes, I wanted to recall Euripides' *Bacchae* with its comic and terrifying vision of the old men girding their dry loins and white hair in ritual garments, then fettling their stiff old limbs out to the Dionysiac rites and orgies. Thus, I hoped that my belly dancers, the Greek solo and line dances, our old crone and her *tsamikos* might recall something of the ancient Attic rituals.

This, in turn, allowed me to give my Chorus of Trees a little eight-line choral song as a coda. Here, for the first time, I dropped the rhythm established at the beginning and, as Whitman did at the end of "Cavalry Crossing a Ford," closed with a new and different movement. If this final stanza *has* a metrical system, I haven't discovered it. It now seems to me that the rhythm of that stanza's first line:

Soon, each one of us will be taken

may echo some of the trochaic or spondaic movements in earlier half-lines. But I had no such *conscious* intention when writing; I merely noted that this rhythm satisfied my ear and questioned it no further.

I *did* discover something odd, though, about the rhythm of the rest of "Old Apple Trees." Once, when I was visiting a small college, a student asked about this poem. Describing its rhythmic basis, I heard myself say, "It goes: di DUM di di DUM DUM; di DUM di di DUM DUM. You know, like that old show tune, 'Heat Wave:' 'We're having a heat wave; a tropical heat wave.'" Later I wondered what could have brought that silly thing into my head; I could just as well have said, "Blues in the Night": "My Mamma done tole' me, when I was in knee pants. . . ." Or, since I've long been a devotee of early music, couldn't I have found an example *there*? After all, why NOT something from *The St. Matthew Passion*?

27

The only time I'd even listened to "Heat Wave" with any attention had been in Saratoga Springs, New York, at a little night place called Jack's—a joint that catered to Black transvestites and had a mostly drag floor show. Just as our Detroit intellectuals haunted the belly dance joints, so the artists and writers from Yaddo haunted Jack's—another respite from the American middle class. The star dancer there was a gorgeous Black stripper who used that "Heat Wave" song for her theme; indeed, she was known, simply, as Heat Wave. All of us, sex-starved by our monastic existence at Yaddo under its dowager queen, tried desperately to start something, anything, with her. In vain—to only one, the dullest, dumpiest among us, would she even talk. For hours, she sat with him discussing the best brand of single-edged blades, while we gnawed our knuckles in frustration.

To have chosen that song when trying to demonstrate the poem's rhythm, though, does suggest that Jack's and that Black dancer were linked in my mind with the belly dance joints in Detroit. One of the best belly dancers there (Princess Sahara, half-Scottish and half-Russian) had married one of my students. The best of all (Princess Baudia, half-North African and half-Kentuckian) was another Black girl, another stunning beauty. It must have been that rhythm that brought such places, such dances and dancers to my mind and to my poem in the first place. It would be nice, now, if I could show the rhythms of the two kinds of dance music to be similar. Too bad; I am familiar with most belly dance drum patterns, and none bears any close resemblance to the rhythm of "Heat Wave."

It seems to me now, though, that this rhythm may have contributed much more. I am convinced that it must have been related all along to a sense of barbarous ritual which I feel in such places—and, perhaps, to a feeling that after a dull and proper youth I, like the old men of Thebes, was having a somewhat riotous old age. I remember once telling my analyst about taking a visiting poet who belonged to a religious order to one of those joints and being amused that, although *he'd* wanted to go there in the first place, he'd become so uncomfortable that he'd had to leave. My analyst asked, "But going to such places—isn't that really *your* religion?" I still don't think I have one but, like much one's analyst says, it was hard to deny.

As for the tune "Heat Wave," it is, after all, about still another dance and dancer, and the most pronounced spondee of all bumps down on the name of that dance:

She started a heat wave, by making her seat wave.
The temperature's rising; it isn't surprising:
She certainly can
Cancan.

I have no doubt that my own spondee, once established in the poem's opening, had brought with it the cancan and the belly dance joints. That leaves me to ask, however, why I had put the spondee there in the first place? The cancan started, of course, in the low dives and brothels of Montmartre. And for all this song's commercial cutiefication and corruption, doesn't it also gesture, in some way, toward the orgiastic and barbarous—which we still see as a celebration of something which, if not holy, will nonetheless destroy us should we, like Pentheus of *The Bacchae*, refuse it worship?

I once owned a record titled *Bach for Percussion* on which a percussion ensemble, led by Saul Goodman, tympanist of the New York Philharmonic, played a number of toccatas and fugues in transcriptions by John Klein. In explanation, the record jacket quoted the musicologist Willi Apel to the effect that it is through their rhythmic, as much as their melodic, interdependence that the voices of a contrapuntal fabric achieve their essential individuality. One should be able, then, to remove a fugue's pitch, its melody, and still have that fugue's architectonic design.

Klein's musical demonstration was exhilarating. I used to play his version of the "Little Fugue in G Minor," for friends, letting them guess what it was. Invariably, they would identify it as Central African tribal music? East Asian? Polynesian? My colleague, Baxter Hathaway, once I'd identified the source, said he couldn't help wondering if all truly great art might not be built on some such deep construct of primitive celebration, covered only by a thin veneer of melody, of reason and civilization. I couldn't help wondering if that might be one more way that art imitates life.

AGAINST YOUR BELIEFS

"Well, now," says Tranter Reuben Dewy, after his wife had complained against the coarseness of a neighbor's tale about "chawing" in time to music, "that sort o' coarse touch . . . is to my mind a recommendation; for it do always prove a story to be true. And for the same reason, I like a story with a bad moral. My sonnies, all true stories have a coarse touch or a bad moral, depend upon't. If the story-tellers could ha' got decency and good morals from true stories, who'd have troubled to invent parables?" I reach much the same notion about poems—true ones are likely to have not only improprieties but, often enough, a bad moral; that is, a meaning counter to the author's conscious beliefs.

In 1868, just four years before Thomas Hardy published *Under the Greenwood Tree* (the source of Tranter Reuben's disquisition), Gerard Manley Hopkins entered the Roman Catholic Society of Jesus. At that time he tried to destroy all his earlier poetry, resolving "to write no more . . . unless by the wish of my superiors." Indeed, it was by his rector's wish that after a break of seven years Hopkins began writing again, finally producing those poems so widely admired today. Surely he, if anyone, should be the artist whose work serves his morality. Admittedly, his beliefs diverge from those of most Christians, certainly of most Jesuits:

INVERSNAID

This darksome burn, horseback brown,
His rollrock highroad roaring down,
In coop and in comb, the fleece of his foam
Flutes and low to the lake falls home.

A windpuff-bonnet of fawn-froth
Turns and twindles over the broth
Of a pool so pitchblack, fell-frowning,
It rounds and rounds despair to drowning.

Degged with dew, dappled with dew
Are the groins of the braes that the brook treads through,
Wiry heathpacks, flitches of fern,
And the beadbonny ash that sits over the burn.

What would the world be, once bereft
Of wet and of wildness? Let them be left,
O let them be left, wildness and wet;
Long live the weeds and the wilderness yet.

Odd sentiments for one dedicated to chastity, poverty and obedience! Poverty sorts ill with such luxurious language while obedience fosters "wildness" as poorly as chastity does groins "Degged with dew." Groins, however we may gloss the word from Welsh or from architectural usage, pretty much remain "groins."

Here, as so often, Hopkins was more influenced by John Duns Scotus, the advocate of "individuation" and "thisness" (*haecceitas*), than by Thomas Aquinas or by Ignatius Loyola's counsel to turn away from the individual and specific to the disciplines of a defined universal. Typically, having rejected his family's Anglicanism and securely ensconced himself in the Roman church, Hopkins chose a philosopher abominated by that church. How better to concretize the struggle between the opposed sides of his nature—a struggle which his friend Robert Bridges characterized as "the naked encounter of sensualism and asceticism"?

We might turn, then, to a poem Hopkins wrote toward the end of his life:

THOU ART INDEED JUST, LORD

Justus quidem tu es, Domine, si disputem tecum;
verumtamen justa loquar ad te: Quare via impiorum,
prosperatur? &c.

Thou art indeed just, Lord, if I contend
With thee; but, sir, so what I plead is just.

Why do sinners' ways prosper? and why must
Disappointment all I endeavour end?

Wert thou my enemy, O thou my friend,
How wouldst thou worse, I wonder than thou dost
Defeat, thwart me? Oh, the sots and thralls of lust
Do in spare hours more thrive than I that spend,

Sir, life upon thy cause. See, banks and brakes
Now leav'ed how thick! lac'ed they are again
With fretty chervil, look, and fresh wind shakes

Them; birds build—but not I build; no, but strain,
Time's eunuch, and not breed one work that wakes.
Mine, O thou lord of life, send my roots rain.

Where Hopkins once had offered us luxuries of language and music, richly echoing sound effects, coinages and hyphenations, eccentric and archaic diction, we now find a sparse and open lexicon. The one oddity of language applies, as before, to the luxuriant plants: "fretty chervil." Other obscurities could rise only from the inverted syntax, which directly represents the speaker's torments in opposed phrases and interjections crossing and countering each other. The earlier poem, despite its lexical riches, had a free flowing, straightforward syntax and the easy bounce of a simple "sprung rhythm." In contrast, the later poem displays a strict iambic pentameter against which the sentence structure and accent placement struggle just as the speaker seems to writhe against the restraints of his monastic existence.

Such frustration is understandable in the voice of a priest whose beliefs were foundering, and this might well lead to a mounting condemnation of the thriving "sinners" and the "sots and thralls of lust." Yet it is startling to identify those recreants: "banks and brakes," the flourishing plants, nesting birds. Unlike Jeremiah, whose complaint the poem's opening translates, Hopkins does not cite those creatures merely as metaphors for wicked humans, betrayers of the God who created and now seemingly fosters them. He

33

condemns the actual plants and birds — the wet and wild beings he once had all-hailed and "Long live[d]." Not only has Hopkins chosen an eccentric and once-outlawed philosophy to express his feelings, that philosophy now expresses not an affirmation but his own despair.

A related clash of attitudes appears throughout Hopkins' work. The consolations of the Golden Echo seem neither more convincing nor more enduring than the anguish of the Leaden Echo. The individuation affirmed in such Scotist poems as "Kingfishers," "Pied Beauty," or "Binsey Poplars" cannot cancel out the despair of such "terrible" sonnets as "I wake and feel the fell of dark, not day" or "Carrion Comfort." Though we recall the confident affirmation of

> Each mortal thing does one thing and the same:
> Deals out that being indoors each one dwells;
> Selves—goes itself; *myself* it speaks and spells,
> Crying *Whát I do is me: for that I came.*

we remember no less the agonized self-loathing of

> I am gall, I am heartburn. . . .
> Selfyeast of spirit a dull dough sours. I see
> The lost are like this, and their scourge to be
> As I am mine, their sweating selves; but worse.

or the exhausted pleading of

> Soul, self; come, poor Jackself, I do advise
> You, jaded, let be; call off thoughts awhile
> Elsewhere; leave comfort root-room; . . .

If that comfort ever came "unforseen times" to light "a lovely mile," it never again brightened Hopkins' poems. Not only has "Inversnaid" proven coarse, these last sonnets have reached a bad moral, come to no good end with their beliefs.

Perhaps we'd have better luck with the skeptic Hardy and a poem that sets out to state his *dis*beliefs:

AFTERWARDS

When the Present has latched its postern behind my
    tremulous stay
And the May month flaps its glad green leaves like wings,
Delicate-filmed as new-spun silk, will the neighbors say,
    "He was a man who used to notice such things"?

If it be in the dusk when, like an eyelid's soundless blink,
    The dewfall-hawk comes crossing the shades to alight
Upon the wind-warped upland thorn, a gazer may think,
    "To him this must have been a familiar sight."

If I pass during some nocturnal blackness, mothy and warm,
    When the hedgehog travels furtively over the lawn,
One may say, "He strove that such innocent creatures
    should come to no harm,
But he could do little for them; and now he is gone."

If, when hearing that I have been stilled at last, they stand
    at the door,
    Watching the full-starred heavens that winter sees,
Will this thought rise on those who will meet my face no
    more,
    "He was one who had an eye for such mysteries"?

And will any say when my bell of quittance is heard in
    the gloom,
    And a crossing breeze cuts a pause in its outrollings,
Till they rise again, as they were a new bell's boom,
    "He hears it not now, but used to notice such things"?

Who could fail to admire such sharp, concrete details? Robert
Lowell once remarked that this poem had 24/20 vision.
    The title, "Afterwards,"refers, of course, to Hardy's convic-
tions about a life after death: in its conscious surface, the poem
admits to no hereafter beyond one's lingering influence on friends

or neighbors—who, if they notice some touching scene or particular beauty in the landscape, may recall the poet's familiarity with, and care for, such matters. Belief in an "afterward" so brief and local would scarcely opiate the masses. This concurs with what we know of the agnostic Hardy, the ecclesiastical architect who loved the church's buildings, its music, the liturgy and ritual, but could not share the supernatural doctrines they promoted.

Still, the poem's underside does little to promote those opinions—isn't it a little inept to depict one's death so incongruously? Hardy has scarcely written a line before slipping into terms at odds with his own conscious disbelief. Need everything be quite so gauzy and dewy? Shouldn't a death promising so little occur in a bleaker month? Why image that moment's leaves as wings? Surely we could invent details more appropriate:

THE END

When the Present has latched its postern behind my
    hesitant stay,
And November flaps its few dead leaves like wings,
Leathery-tough, of small black bats, will the neighbors say,
    "He was a man who used to notice such things"?

If Hardy's life had been tremulous and leaf-like, death certainly needn't occur just when leaves are being reborn, not merely trembling, but expensive, delicate and new-spun, green and glad.

In Hardy's second stanza, death arrives, expectably, as a raptor. My bird book, however, displays no creature so delicately crepuscular as a "dewfall hawk." Besides, though death *is* associated with the closing of eyes, shouldn't that last longer than a blink?

If it be in the dusk when, as an eye might forever close,
    The sharp-clawed hawk comes out of deepening shades
        to dive

Onto the wind-warped upland thorn, a witness might
   suppose,
   "He must have often seen such sights when alive."

Next, as nonbelievers, shouldn't we banish the womb-like
warmth and softness from Hardy's last moments? And, certainly,
the suggestions—the guilt by angelic association—of moths with
the soul? Hardy implicitly compared this life to a hedghog's scurry
across a clearing in the wastes of unrecorded time— crawling out of
a hole at one edge of the lawn, then back into another hole in the
earth, a grave. This accords with Hardy's disbeliefs, yet, lest his
benevolence might suggest some sentimental response toward a
secular and coldly neutral universe, we should surely rewrite to
underline death's permanence:

If I die during some night's utter blackness, sterile and chill,
   When the house cat slips out, prowling for prey through
   the wood,
   One may say, "He strove that all creatures might live one
   with Nature still,
   Yet great forests get cleared; now he, too, is gone for good."

Almost at once, Hardy's poem backslides, lifting its eyes
toward the heights. If we cannot quite abolish that gaze, at least we
can diminish its mystical tone, the glance toward the eternal—those
"heavens" which become "full-starred" with the poet's death:

If, sometime after I have died, they stand at the door
   Watching the sky's blank, bleak space that winter sees,
   Will it occur to those who will meet my face no more,
   "He was one who had an eye for sights like these."

Above all, mustn't we banish such crucificial terms as thorns
and crossings, whether of hawks or belltones? Shouldn't we wipe
out all hints of resurrection—that the speaker's face might "rise"
even in his neighbors' thoughts, that the bell's sounds might "rise
again as they were a new bell's boom?" Of course a poet can be

figured as a sort of bell or mouth; arguably, the passage could refer only to Hardy's continuing fame despite being "stilled at last." Yet, surely, his context suggests more that:

> And will any say when my death bell's tolling is heard in
>   the gloom
> Till its sound is silenced by a quick shift of the breeze,
> Though they may hear some different bell's more distant
>   boom,
> "He hears it not now and, in time, all live things cease."

Thus: the orthodox skeptic's poem, acceptable even to the high priests of doubt!

Meantime, of course, we have lost a masterpiece. I have driven out precisely the qualities I admire in Hardy: the complexity of attitude, the richness of mind which lets us accept, not his ideas, but *him*, the man whose work embodies so many of our hopes and doubts, reasonings and contradictions. Further, Hardy creates those complexities in the simplest, most direct language; "The Oxen" springs at once to mind. As does "Channel Firing," with its somewhat easy dismissal and mockery of war, only to turn in the last stanza:

> Again the guns disturbed the hour,
> Roaring their readiness to avenge,
> As far inland as Stourton Tower,
> And Camelot, and starlit Stonehenge.

As the echoes of those guns (preparing for World War I) pass inland, they also pass backward in time to the fortifications of our prehistoric and mythical past. With each step, war becomes more romantic and inspiring. That, no doubt, will offend those who would draft all resources, including poetry, for the war against war. To me, it seems better that poetry help wake us to our dilemma: we find war terrible, but we love it. Why else have we had so much of it? How can we restrain dread desires if we don't admit they are ours?

Reconsidering our discussion of Hopkins and the diction he chose for his later poem, "Thou Art Indeed Just, Lord," it would seem that a simpler language surface tends either to indicate or to promote a more complex attitude. Conversely, elaborate language often betrays and assists simplified attitudes—uncritical acceptance of beliefs we might otherwise question. How often are an elevated or obscure language, musical phrasings, even nonsense passages, a basic component of cheerleading, of political demonstrations, of religious ceremonies. Such language brings us nearer the condition of a child who understands little of the language's denotation, but who must gauge the drift of its intent from tone and music or risk the loss of comfort, of nurture, even of life. Consistency is (and should be) the bugaboo of small minds; without it, they would perish.

If we've fared so poorly among the skeptics, perhaps we can do better among the heretics. Could D. H. Lawrence, the prophet of sexual fulfillment, offer more consistency? Certainly, his dogmas— or, as with most saviors, the popular *mis*understanding of his doctrine—have gained much ground against Christianity; sexual salvation may, indeed, be the rough beast slouching toward our Bethlehem to be born. Yet Lawrence's most anthologized poem offers little reassurance:

PIANO

Softly, in the dusk, a woman is singing to me;
Taking me back down the vista of years, till I see
A child sitting under the piano, in the boom of the
    tingling strings
And pressing the small, poised feet of a mother who
    smiles as she sings.

In spite of myself, the insidious mastery of song
Betrays me back, till the heart of me weeps to belong
To the old Sunday evenings at home, with winter outside
And hymns in the cosy parlour, the tinkling piano our
    guide.

> So now it is vain for the singer to burst into clamour
> With the great black piano appassionato. The glamour
> Of childish days is upon me, my manhood is cast
> Down in the flood of remembrance, I weep like a child for
> the past.

If we hoped for eroticism, we find an unseemly propriety, an inappropriate chastity. Lawrence yields us not even one "coarse touch." If we wanted violets woven amongst the pubic hair, we get a scene from a Hallmark card: "the old Sunday evenings at home . . . hymns in the cosy parlour, the tinkling piano our guide." Worse, the speaker is insidiously betrayed by the glamour (i.e., in Scots, the evil magic) of childhood; the memory of his mother's music prevents any response to the woman now singing "appassionato" to him in the twilight—though, in an earlier version, that woman's "wild Hungarian air" had won out. Now, the speaker's "manhood is cast / Down," and, in place of any more appropriate fluid, he can produce only tears. Need our sexual emancipator present such a specter of impotence?

Allen Ginsberg has been our prophet of gay acceptance, celebrant of "alcohol and cock and balls," of those who "let themselves be fucked in the ass by saintly motorcyclists and screamed for joy"—attitudes perhaps comparable to Hopkins' praise for "wildness and wet" or for "the weeds and the wilderness." Yet if Ginsberg's best known shorter poem (which I find far more successful than the longer, more famous pieces) displays less of loss and anguish than do Hopkins' "terrible" sonnets, that is only because its speaker has already submitted to proscription and solitude.

A SUPERMARKET IN CALIFORNIA

What thoughts I have of you tonight, Walt Whitman, for I walked down the streets under the trees with a headache self-conscious looking at the full moon.

In my hungry fatigue, and shopping for images, I went into the neon fruit supermarket, dreaming of your enumerations!

What peaches and what penumbras! Whole families shopping at night! Aisles full of husbands! Wives in the avocados, babies in the tomatoes!—and you, Garcia Lorca, what were you doing down by the watermelons?

I saw you, Walt Whitman, childless, lonely old grubber, poking among the meats in the refrigerator and eyeing the grocery boys.

I heard you asking questions of each: Who killed the pork chops? What price bananas? Are you my Angel?

I wandered in and out of the brilliant stacks of cans following you, and followed in my imagination by the store detective.

We strode down the open corridors together in our solitary fancy tasting artichokes, possessing every frozen delicacy, and never passing the cashier.

Where are we going, Walt Whitman? The doors close in an hour. Which way does your beard point tonight?

(I touch your book and dream of our odyssey in the supermarket and feel absurd.)

Will we walk all night through solitary streets? The trees add shade to shade, lights out in the houses, we'll both be lonely.

Will we stroll dreaming of the lost America of love past blue automobiles in driveways, home to our silent cottage?

Ah, dear father, graybeard, lonely old courage-teacher, what America did you have when Charon quit poling his ferry and you got out on a smoking bank and stood watching the boat disappear on the black waters of Lethe?

Where are the orgies of yesteryear, the conviction that screams of joy would lead to "the lost America of love"? Instead, we find the poet, surely aware of the nastier slang associations, in California's "neon fruit supermarket." Even there he is surrounded by "whole families . . . husbands . . . wives . . . babies"—those less alone and perhaps less subject to self-conscious headaches. Here, too, he encounters his homosexual poetic forebears: Garcia Lorca, who supplied the form and verbal pattern for one section of "Howl," and Walt Whitman, the "childless, lonely old grubber, poking among the [cold] meats" and looking for an Angel among the grocery boys—who will become the poet's "dear father" and "lonely old courage-teacher."

We should not let the bright lights and vegetable abundance of the poem's opening blind us to its ultimate desolation. All that produce, the "wives in the avocados, babies in the tomatoes," are merely the visions of Tantalus. For all the supermarket's plenty, the basic thirsts and hungers remain unslaked, unsatisfied—the frozen delicacies are tasted only in fancy. The poet never "pass[es] the cashier," apparently unwilling or unable to pay the price, and is "followed in [his] imagination by the store detective." That sense of guilt leads directly to scenes of punishment and sterility. Outside, the trees "add shade to shade," and the odyssey remains "solitary" (the word appears twice, "lonely," thrice); its goal is not Ithaca but the "silent cottage" and the "black waters." In place of any "lost America of love," the poet imagines a scene which recalls Dante's encounter, on the burning sands of the *Inferno's* Seventh Circle, with his own teacher and paternal imago, Ser Brunetto Latini, lewdly dancing among the sodomites under raining flakes of fire. Small wonder that when Whitman debarks on that "smoking bank," Ginsberg changes the river from the Styx to Lethe—the river of oblivion.

In English, the nearest thing to a Dante is John Milton, who certainly demanded that poetry and belief be united. Yet today few even of those Christians who could adhere to Milton's dogmas read his God's self-justifications except as a religious or academic duty. Those who read Milton for enjoyment do so for the realized character of Satan—Milton, of course, had experienced the delights of overthrowing high authority. And while it may be right for sin to be so attractive—why else has it given us so much trouble?—that doesn't excuse God for being a sophistical bore. Which should remind us that even with Dante, we read and reread the *Inferno*; few reread more than selections from the *Purgatorio* or *Paradiso*—passages marked by transforming imagery or sonority, not by the doctrines they expound.

The most influential recent Christian poet is T. S. Eliot, who constantly declared that poems must be written out of a traditional and established system of belief. Yet, by the time Eliot managed to lull his sexuality into settling for doctrine, his poems had lost tension and interest. At least for this reader, the liturgical cadences of *Four Quartets* will never match the anguished human dilemma of "Prufrock." I find much the same of Theodore Roethke's later mysticism: it may have numbed the pain of individuation and self-hood, "that old agony of the specific," but thereby it weakened the poems. If not an opiate, such mysticism was a sort of mental aspirin which did not cure the distress and sorrows of existence, but only made them vague and indefinite.

If Ginsberg, the spokesman for acts which others declared "unnatural," disappoints us, such "Nature" poets as Frost, or even Wordsworth, prove no more consistent. Who knows a poem more fearful of Nature, that supposedly benign deity, than

> No motion has she now, no force;
>   She neither hears nor sees,
> Rolled round in Earth's diurnal course
>   With rocks and stones and trees!

or than

> The woods around it have it; it is theirs.
> All animals are smothered in their lairs.

or than the buzz saw world of "Out, Out"?

Neither can we resort to Ginsberg's models, William Carlos Williams or Whitman. For years, Williams preached literary and sexual freedom. Yet he is at his best in a poem clearly surprised and delighted by a scene of Victorian, if not downright Puritan, purity.

NANTUCKET

> Flowers through the window
> lavender and yellow

43

changed by white curtains—
Smell of cleanliness—

Sunshine of late afternoon—
On the glass tray

a glass pitcher, the tumbler
turned down, by which

a key is lying—And the
immaculate white bed

Again and again, Williams had admonished us: "Write American, not English!" Yet his last great poem, "Of Asphodel," a marvelous work composed after several heart attacks, not only proclaims his deep-set fidelity to the wife his earlier poems must have injured, but does so in a language which could almost pass for Tennyson:

Of asphodel, that greeny flower,
    like a buttercup
        upon its branching stem—
I come to sing, my love, to you.

Can't we at least demand loyalty to one's own literary doctrines?
    Or we may turn to the "dear father" many see as as progenitor of Ginsberg's verse? A story used to circulate that Roethke once, while teaching a class at the University of Washington, reached for a copy of *Leaves of Grass* to prove a point he was making. Picking a passage at random, he happened to read the fifth section of "Song of Myself":

I believe in you my soul, the other I am must not abase
    itself to you,
And you must not be abased to the other.

Loafe with me on the grass, loose the stop from your
    throat,

44

Not words, not music or rhyme I want, not custom or
lecture, not even the best.
Only the lull I like, the hum of your valv'ed voice.

I mind how once we lay such a transparent summer
morning,
How you settled your head athwart my hips and gently
turn'd over upon me,
And parted the shirt from my bosom-bone, and plunged
your tongue to my bare stript heart,
And reach'd till you felt my beard, and reach'd till you
held my feet.

Swiftly arose and spread around me the peace and
knowledge that pass all the argument of the earth,
And I know that the hand of God is the promise of my own,
And I know that the spirit of God is the brother of my own,
And that all the men ever born are also my brothers, and
the women my sisters and lovers,

And that a kelson of the creation is love,
And limitless are leaves stiff or drooping in the fields,
And brown ants in the little wells beneath them,
And mossy scabs of the worm fence, heap'd stones, elder,
mullein and poke-weed.

Roethke looked up suddenly, said, "Wait a minute!" and pored
over the passage again. His eyes wide with shock, he looked up and
exclaimed, "Jesus Christ! He's sucking him off!" That, of course,
scandalized the campus and helped propel a notice of dismissal
which administrators had to quietly recover from the campus mails
when they learned that Roethke had just been awarded both the
National Book Award and the Pulitzer Prize.

Perhaps too good a story to be factual, but certain truths do
lurk there—about the openness of universities to original insight,
about how even the brightest may be blind to what their society
wishes to obscure. At that time, readers as able as Roethke were

often oblivious to Whitman's sexuality and read such passages without discerning what was depicted or intended.

Most serious readers of Whitman are now aware of his sexual orientation and that, lest he see himself as shut out from his society, indeed from the company of the blessed, he had constructed a doctrine, political and metaphysical, of inclusion—a process I will later detail in "Whitman's Self-Song." Long before others did, Whitman recognized links between homosexuality and democracy, between orgiastic pleasure and religious exaltation. By rather simple extensions of accepted political and religious tenets, he devised not only a political platform of "adhesion" but also a vision of mystical union with God, and with the totality of existence, through forbidden sexual acts. Isolated by what James Merrill has described as his only "delight and comfort," Whitman became a worshipper of Pan, of unity with the All.

Yet just as Hopkins had come to wail,

> Comforter, where is your comforting;
> Mary, mother of us, where is your relief?

doctrine could not hold Whitman's despair long at bay. Though his poems continued to celebrate the passing relationship, the god's occasional and unexpected visits, and equally his own freedom to pass on to other scenes and new companions, Whitman's diaries and daybooks reveal both the agonies of pursuing those unwilling and his torment at losing some specific lover. In his later collection, *Sea-Drift*, Whitman becomes one of the "fierce old mother['s] . . . castaways":

> Chaff, straw, splinters of wood, weeds and the sea-gluten,
> Scum, scales from shining rocks, leaves of salt-lettuce, left
>   by the tide,

The ecstatic enumerations of "Song of Myself" are replaced by a listing of

> Me and mine, loose windrows, little corpses,
> Froth, snowy white, and bubbles,

(See, from my dead lips the ooze exuding at last,
See, the prismatic colors glistening and rolling,)
Tufts of straw, sands, fragments,

What had once beckoned to an ecstatic acceptance of life, now calls him toward

Death, death, death, death, death.

Much like the ideational disenchantment we found in Hopkins, Whitman's most beautiful poem, "Out of the Cradle," embodies the same beliefs, but with diametrically opposed emotional polarities, as those of the earlier "Song of Myself." It's pertinent, too, that our greatest poet, who surely would have rejected nearly all we have become, should partially recognize the failure of his own idea system, however grand and daring, either to predict or describe his people's destiny or to cope with his own desolation. Despair as a man, as a political and religious thinker, fueled Whitman's triumph in a field he professed to scorn: literature.

It is surprising, however, and of far-reaching implication, that when Whitman, like Hopkins, moved from a poem of joyous belief to one of anguished questioning, he also moved from a loose and open metric to one more rigid and demanding. In "Song of Myself," with its doctrine of inclusion—inclusion of all forbidden subject matter, of all levels of language and vocabulary, of all modes of image and sound texture—a polymorphous perverse prosody was appropriate. Rather than pick a verse form and stay constant to that, Whitman could promiscuously sample the sounds of all metrical or nonmetrical forms. For "Out of the Cradle," the later, despairing poem, with its recognition that the world was far more chaotic and cruel than were dreamed of in his philosophy, he needed a more fixed form. Since he had failed at, and so rejected, the traditional forms (just as he had rejected conventional sexuality), he had to invent for himself that new verse form. So he came, in a process detailed in my first chapter, to build an elaborate structure of rhythmic variants, giving his poem its musical main frame and definition. Unlike many who, given new freedoms, turn aimless

47

and flabby, Whitman placed his demands upon himself, creating a new form. And having failed to do that in terms of political practice or religious acceptance, he did so triumphantly in the music of a masterpiece which manifested his ideational and sexual failure.

I have elsewhere quoted John Jay Chapman's remark that anything you've believed more than three weeks is a lie. (Hardy's case suggests that the same is true of disbeliefs!) I've also noted a Cornell University study which demonstrated that those with strong political, philosophical, or religious convictions were less aware of the world around them; preserving those ideas demands protection from corrosive fact. A truly active mind, Chapman thought, should notice, within three weeks, just how little of this world fits into even the broadest and bravest schema.

Adolf Hitler, in contrast, boasted that he was one of the "great simplifiers." It's true that few have been so able to simplify their world simply by destroying what didn't fit their yearning to define and control. We are sometimes more successful with thought processes. Recent studies of the brain show that its dominant and analytical left side not only simplifies but quite willingly fabricates facts to render its theories acceptable. Unaware of those deceptions, it assumes that what fits its rationale must in fact be the case, suppressing information not conducive to a unified and orderly view. How swiftly logic turns to propaganda!

Robert Frost once said that for problems which have answers, we go to medicine or law; for a problem with none, we go to poetry. (After all, if it *has* an answer, is it much of a problem?) Elsewhere, he asserted:

> It is but a fake poem, and no poem at all if the best of
> it was thought of first and saved for the last. . . . No
> surprise for the writer, no surprise for the reader.

Discovery is always a surprise, so the poem favors the multiplicity of our perceptions and feelings over the simplifications of our system-building. After decades of empire, it's natural that Americans demand their lives be made still freer, simpler, easier—regardless of the cost to others or their own development. Their poetry, too, must be easy for everyone to write and must prove reality manage-able and comfy. William Empson wrote, "You don't want chaos and the whole thing there."

But W. H. Auden counters: "Poetry makes nothing happen." It surely makes life no simpler or easier. Except that, if you can jar your mind awake every three weeks or so, it may surprise itself by a discovery and so become better prepared for the world's and its own contradictions. Most brands of Christianity hold that the test of faith is not the absence of doubt but its management. The broader the assertion of absolute certainty, the greater the likelihood that it was made to conceal knowledge of evidence to the contrary. If neither Socrates nor Whitehead, Spinoza nor Kant could make the world line up and hold still, our chances are less than impressive. Still, one of our intermittent glories is that we go on trying.

To paraphrase the good Tranter Reuben: Depend upon't, my sonnies, every grand affirmation entails some excluded possibility or distasteful conclusion. Why else would anyone be to the trouble of devising metaphysical systems or the consolation of religious certainty?

SHAPES MERGING AND EMERGING

To suggest that perfection may not readily be improved, I used to give students a copy of William Wordsworth's "She Dwelt Among the Untrodden Ways" together with my own intentionally corrupted version:

> She dwelt among the untrodden ways
>   Beside the springs of Dove,
> A maid whom there were none to praise
>   And very few to love;
>
> A violet by a mossy stone
>   Half hidden from the eye!
> —Fair as a star, when only one
>   Is shining in the sky.
>
> She lived unknown, and few could know
>   When Lucy ceased to be;
> But she is in her grave, and, oh,
>   The difference to me!

> She lived among the untravelled ways
>   Beside the hills of Glove,
> A maid whom any girl might praise
>   And any man would love;
>
> Fair as a rose beside a stone
>   Half hidden from the eye!
> —The fairest star that anyone
>   Could see in all the sky.

She dwelt unheard-of, few could know
That she was dead, but she
Is sleeping her last sleep, and, oh,
How great a loss to me!

No less to English literature!

After noting the more obvious outrages of my version and so hinting at the shining validity of Wordsworth's, I usually turned to the second stanza, focusing on the poem's deeper workings. Wordsworth found so apt an image for Lucy that he could say she *was* (not only was *like*) a violet—retiring, natural to woodland paths and secluded mossy springs. My substituted rose changes her into something cultivated for display, manufactured, possibly vinyl. His poem's "untrodden ways" ("tread" being the sexual verb for birds) intensifies the purity suggested by "Dove," the name of the nearby springs. My stand-in, Lucy the Beauty Queen, seems less virginal than hard to get; my fulsome endorsement seems to reflect little but our usual unctuousness toward those recently dead. Meantime, the imagery's development from obscurity to grandeur has been broken down. To call *my* Lucy "fair as a star" yields no growth of insight or perception; after my first stanza's praise, the only progression possible would be some discovery that she's a cheat and a fraud.

That rose, though, is misplaced in more far-reaching ways. A violet, its four petals glowing softly in a shaded, mossy corner, is easily transfigured into a star with four rays lighting the evening sky. A rose's brighter, clustering petals invite no such metamorphosis. Wordsworth's recognition of a starlike radiance in this simple flower parallels his recognition of constant purity in a girl so unpretentious and unacclaimed; the visual link argues a sound character appraisal.

Further valuable effects have been damaged or discarded. Wordsworth's violet grows "by a mossy stone / Half-hidden from the eye." My rose stands "*beside* a stone / Half-hidden from the eye"—evidently a short-stemmed boutonniere abutting some veritable boulder! Not only is the size relationship lost, but so is the mossiness, which might carry associations with burials and

52

gravesites. We also lose a vital ambiguity: "by" implies not only "near" but also "because of." The original punctuation urges this latter implication—a violet half-hidden *by means of* a mossy stone.

Lifting the flower from beneath the stone, Wordsworth elevates it to the heavens—the very emblem of steadfast virtue. Yet his star's solitary splendor carries a peculiar irony: it is probably the evening star, the harbinger of night and darkness. And it is hurled, almost at once, back underneath what is now undeniably a gravestone. We have dared say that "She lived . . ." (as opposed to the opening, "She dwelt . . .") only when almost able to admit that she has died; to have uttered her starlike, simple but luminous name (missing from my version), only to see that star flash out; to have spoken the euphemistic "ceased to be" only to arrive at the flat declaration that "she is in her grave." This climax of language texture, the effort to voice an unbearable reality through increasingly straightforward, unpoetic language, coincides precisely with the climax in the image structure as the star is hurled back into darkness.

This climax is further underscored by the poem's strongest metrical effect—the near-failure of two stresses in the climactic line:

> But she is in her grave . . .

To stay and steady itself, that line rushes on to some heavy syllable, only to reach the most arresting, gravest of syllables: "grave." (In contrast, the cheery bounce of Wordsworth's first version, "But now she's in her grave," drains force from that word and from the exclamatory "oh.") All three technical factors—imagery, language texture and metrical force—converge here in the poem's climax. To alter the flower's shape or to strip the moss from the stone, as my version does, dismantles the substructure of images which, like the invisible main beams of a house, determine form and function.

A similar example of visual images yoked together not by violence but by great mental and emotional energy is to be found in Edwin Arlington Robinson:

53

MR. FLOOD'S PARTY

Old Eben Flood, climbing alone one night
Over the hill between the town below
And the forsaken upland hermitage
That held as much as he should ever know
On earth again of home, paused warily.
The road was his with not a native near;
And Eben, having leisure, said aloud,
For no man else in Tilbury Town to hear:

"Well, Mr. Flood, we have the harvest moon
Again, and we may not have many more;
The bird is on the wing, the poet says,
And you and I have said it here before.
Drink to the bird." He raised up to the light
The jug that he had gone so far to fill,
And answered huskily: "Well, Mr. Flood,
Since you propose it, I believe I will."

Alone, as if enduring to the end
A valiant armor of scarred hopes outworn,
He stood there in the middle of the road
Like Roland's ghost winding a silent horn.
Below him, in the town among the trees,
Where friends of other days had honored him,
A phantom salutation of the dead
Rang thinly till old Eben's eyes were dim.

Then, as a mother lays her sleeping child
Down tenderly, fearing it may awake,
He set the jug down slowly at his feet
With trembling care, knowing that most things break;
And only when assured that on firm earth
It stood, as the uncertain lives of men
Assuredly did not, he paced away,
And with his hand extended paused again:

"Well, Mr. Flood, we have not met like this
In a long time; and many a change has come
To both of us, I fear, since last it was
We had a drop together. Welcome home!"
Convivially returning with himself,
Again he raised the jug up to the light;
And with an acquiescent quaver said:
"Well, Mr. Flood, if you insist, I might.

"Only a very little, Mr. Flood—
For auld lang syne. No more, sir; that will do."
So, for the time, apparently it did,
And Eben evidently thought so too;
For soon amid the silver loneliness
Of night he lifted up his voice and sang,
Secure, with only two moons listening,
Until the whole harmonious landscape rang—

"For auld lang syne." The weary throat gave out,
The last word wavered; and the song was done.
He raised again the jug regretfully
And shook his head, and was again alone.
There was not much that was ahead of him,
And there was nothing in the town below—
Where strangers would have shut the many doors
That many friends had opened long ago.

There is an obvious visual similarity between a warrior lifting a horn to his lips (the hero of *The Song of Roland*, commanding the rear guard, was given Charlemagne's oliphant, or ivory horn, to summon help if attacked) and someone hoisting a liquor jug to his mouth. And a delightful incongruity lies in comparing Robinson's half-crocked old codger to the romantic, half-mythical Roland, ambushed and killed by the Moors at Roncesvalles in 778 A.D.

Once again, those linked shapes implicitly compare traits of character. Like many heroes, Roland was not only admirable but self-centered, causing his own and others' deaths. Prideful, he refused to blow the horn until too late; Charlemagne returned to find only his knights' bodies. Though Eben has suffered many "hopes outworn," Robinson's canny syntax tell us that what he endures to the end is not scorn or neglect, but his own armor. Too proud to call for aid, he turns to drunkenness and double vision, conjuring up a company of selves who treat him as a returning celebrity. Although the narrator calls him by the nickname "Eben," he addresses himself as "Mr. Flood."

This self-destructive pride resounds throughout the poem. Eben is glad to find himself "with not a native near" so that "secure, with only two moons listening" he can speak "For no man else in Tilbury Town to hear." He is excluded not by the villagers but by his self-indulgent fantasy of being treated as a dignitary, or as a child who mustn't be wakened from his dream. His tone toward the whole village is finally contemptuous and dismissive:

> And there was nothing in the town below—
> Where strangers would have shut the many doors
> That many friends had opened long ago.

Poignant lines, though they hold a darker revelation: the mere closing of doors against the evening damp, chilliness, burglars, is taken by Eben—as if he did not close his own door—as an affront, so deepening his isolation. Our awareness of his complicity in his defeat helps stave off some narrower, more sentimental reading.

Against Mr. Flood, weary, already self-defeated, withdrawn and withdrawing in Robinson's measured, finely modulated poem, I want to oppose the figure of the cocky young cyclist in a rambunctious piece by Mona Van Duyn:

WHAT THE MOTORCYCLE SAID

Br-r-r-am-m-m, rackety-am-m, **OM**, *Am*:
All—r-r-room, r-r-ram, ala-bas-ter—
Am, the world's my oyster.

I hate plastic, wear it black and slick
hate hardhats, wear one on my head,
that's what the motorcycle said.

Passed phonies in Fords, knocked down billboards, landed
on the other side of The Gap, and Whee,
bypassed history.

When I was born (The Past), baby knew best.
They shook when I bawled, took Freud's path,
threw away their wrath.

R-r-rackety-am-m, *Am*. War, rhyme,
soap, meat, marriage, the Phantom Jet
are shit, and like that.

Hate pompousness, punishment, patience, am into Love,
hate middle-class moneymakers, live on Dad,
that's what the motorcycle said.

Br-r-ramm-m-m. It's Nowsville, man. Passed Oldies,
    Uglies,
Straighties, Honkies. I'll never be
mean, tired or unsexy.

Passed cigarette suckers, souses, mother-fuckers,
losers, went back to Nature and found
how to get VD, stoned.

Passed a cow, too fast to hear her moo, "*I* rolled
our leaves of grass into one ball.
I am the grassy All."

Br-r-ram-m-m, rackety-am-m, **OM**, *Am:*
All—gr-r-rin, oooohgah, gl-l-utton—
Am, the world's my smilebutton.

The poem seems dedicated to downright rattle and clatter, not only in direct imitations of the machine's racket, but in its own heavy alliterations and off-beat rhyming. (The internal rhyme patterns may have been derived from Marianne Moore, though one hesitates to imagine her response to such a poem!) And some of that noise is surprisingly sense-laden. The bike itself produces the mantric sound of Eastern meditation, OM, with its pursuit of selflessness. Accordingly, it bursts past passivity's archtype, a (possibly holy) cow, which claims oneness with the "grassy All" of creation. Thus, in part, the poem seems almost a parody of "What the Thunder Said" in *The Waste Land*, with its seemingly senseless vocables, "Datta. Dayadhvam. Damyata. / Shantih shantih shantih." Just as often, however, the engine blurts the insistant verb of Western individuation, Am, with its drive for total activity, selfhood and selfishness. Environed by these sounds and defined by their oppositions, the rider zooms forth in conventional rebelliousness, full of hate and scorn for others, praise for himself and—though familiar with Freud, Whitman, and Marvell—an appalling insensitivity.

Amidst all this assertive hubbub, however, the poem opens and closes with a visual effect—precisely the sort of juxtaposed image we found in Robinson. The third line holds the poem's first complete bit of syntax: "the world's my oyster." For this cyclist, All is his own—especially should its shape happen to be vaginal—to pry open and enjoy. This image is balanced by the last line, where the closed gray oyster is turned into a vast, grinning smilebutton—the logo of a man so pleased by his own cheerful aggression that he can't imagine the world is not equally delighted. He could run you down, proposition your wife, break your child's arm and glasses, then drive off shouting, "Have a nice day!" and believe he meant it. Nothing better sums him up than the juxtaposition of those two images of his world.

II.

The relation between visual images may affect, as we've seen, not only our sense of a poem's characters and actions; it may also define its structure in much the same way that related shapes or implicit geometric forms—triangles, circles, spirals, crossed diagonals—may give form to a painting. The images we've noted—violet and star, horn and jug, oyster and smilebutton—have all been visually conspicuous in a way that a painting's organizing shapes seldom need be. Still, in a poem, one of the juxtaposed images may well remain immanent and ghostly, demanding imaginative vigor from a reader. We find an example in Sir Thomas Wyatt:

THEY FLEE FROM ME

They flee from me that sometime did me seek,
With naked foot stalking in my chamber.
I have seen them gentle, tame, and meek
That now are wild and do not remember
That sometime they put themself in danger
To take bread at my hand, and now they range
Busily seeking with a continual change.

Thankèd be fortune, it hath been otherwise,
Twenty times better, but once in special:
In thin array, after a pleasant guise,
When her loose gown from her shoulders did fall
And she me caught in her arms long and small;
Therewith all sweetly did me kiss,
And softly said, "Dear heart, how like you this?"

It was no dream; I lay broad waking.
But all is turnèd through my gentleness
Into a strange fashion of forsaking;
And I have leave to go, of her goodness,
And she also to use newfangleness.

But since that I so kindèly am servèd,
I would fain know what she hath deservèd.

For many years we knew this poem only in a corrupted version from Richard Tottel's *Miscellany*. Recovery of the original, begun in the 1920s when Agnes Kate Foxwell discovered Wyatt's manuscripts, shows literary scholarship at its most exciting and consequential. The restored poem came to influence many fine poets, Robert Lowell not least among them.

Tottel's travesty, whether committed by himself or by some hired poetaster, tried to force Wyatt's strenuously expressive rhythms—probably following Italian models—into the rigid Iambics fashionable to a later generation. This diluted not only Wyatt's strenuous tone and music, but even his basic structure of images.

THE LOVER SHOWETH HOW HE IS ABANDONED OF SUCH AS HE ONE TIME ENJOYED

They flee from me that sometime did me seek
With naked foot stalking within my chamber.
Once have I seen them, gentle, tame and meek
That now are wild and do not once remember
That sometime they have put themselves in danger
To take bread at my hand. But now they range
Busily seeking with a continual change.

Thankèd be fortune it hath been otherwise,
Twenty times better. But once especial
In thin array, after a pleasant guise,
When her loose gown did from her shoulder fall
And she me caught in her arms long and small
And therewithal so sweetly did me kiss
And softly said, Dear heart, how like you this?

It was no dream for I lay broad awaking.
But all is turned, now, through my gentleness

Into a bitter fashion of forsaking
And I have leave to go of her goodness
And she also to use newfangledness
But since that I unkindly so am servèd,
How like you this, what hath she now deservèd?

Tottel's explanatory title takes us for obtuse, his reconstituted poem for tone-deaf, offering reportage and smug certainty in place of Wyatt's powerfully conflicted emotion.

I have seen them gentle, tame, and meek,

emphasizing *seen*, implies "I know that this sounds improbable, but . . ." To add the syllable "Once" merely reiterates what we should already know—that the change is regrettable. Wyatt's grand line of loss and emptiness,

That now are wild and do not remember

has, really, only two full stresses; to add a second superfluous "once" renders it impotent. Could anyone read "and do not once remember" without stamping their foot in petulance? Wyatt's most powerful line,

It was no dream; I lay broad waking

where bunched stresses give even more sense of trying to convince oneself of improbable wonders, is ironed flat:

It was no dream for I lay broad awaking.

Whoever said that might as well go back to sleep!
Still, the grossest atrocities have been worked upon the ending—most obviously in the last line, where Wyatt's deep perplexity is replaced by a facetious quip. His wondering question still rings on because we'll never find its answer. Even more enervating is the change of "kindèly" to "unkindly" in the next-to-

last line. As usual, Tottel tells us only what we've always known: a lover finds rejection unkind. We lose not only Wyatt's bitter sarcasm, but also the richnesses of "kindèly." In one sense, the speaker *was* served kindly: sexually, according to the "act of kind," and naturally, "according to one's kind, one's species or type." When Hamlet calls Claudius "a little more than kin and less than kind," he is not impugning his uncle's tenderness but his conformity to natural law.

This leads back to the poem's opening with its "naked foot / Stalking in my chamber"—clearly a beast's foot. Given the suggestions of "stalking" and "range," most readers (even with Tottel's weaker rhythms) imagine a predator, a lioness or leopard. The speaker clearly perceived that—why else *try* to tame her, get her to take bread like a domestic animal? How, then, can he now claim that she should be punished? If she, instead, turned and caught *him*, then mocked his delight, he could scarcely deny that delight. And, since he was too gentle to control such a creature, she *did* treat him "kindèly"—according to her nature and his own.

Yet "gentleness" carries a further irony: the lady (quite possibly Anne Boleyn) "ranged" abroad because Wyatt was *not* sufficiently gentle, that is, "highborn." Given Wyatt's lower station at court, to have sought him even once meant violating that court's "new-fangled" Machievellian manners, its predatory immorality, thus putting herself "in danger"—that is, liable to others' scorn. She might well claim, then, to have treated him "kindèly," even generously. For such a couple, what could exist beyond a brief coupling, then "leave to go"? Still, if reason argues thus, emotion no less craves revenge. This conflict gives the poem its surcharge of complex feelings; Tottel's adulteration into one-sided emotion yields merely a rhymed jingle, a pleasant toy.

Scholars of art history may be even more assiduous than their literary counterparts in tracing allusions to earlier works. This may seem surprising: a knowledge of such antecedents, though enriching, isn't usually *necessary* for appreciating a painting or piece of sculpture. In a poem, though, especially if one term of a central comparison is less explicit, such references may be essential to understanding. Robert Frost's "Spring Pools" is built around a comparison so guarded that, unless we catch literary echoes, we may miss the visual link and the poem's whole point.

SPRING POOLS

These pools that, though in forests, still reflect
The total sky almost without defect
And, like the flowers beside them, chill and shiver,
Will like the flowers beside them soon be gone
And yet not out by any brook or river
But up by roots to bring dark foliage on.

The trees that have it in their pent-up buds
To darken nature and be summer woods,
Let them think twice before they use their powers
To blot out and drink up and sweep away
These flowery waters and these watery flowers
From snow that melted only yesterday.

On first reading, this seemed to me like a verse by some trinomial lady in a local newspaper. Yet disquiets persisted: why should those flowers "chill and shiver"? Even though we may see less direct sunlight if we walk in the woods once the leaves are out, does summer really "darken nature"? Again, why imagine leaf buds to be "pent-up" or the trees possessed of such a rage to destroy? In time, the poem came to seem like a drop of pure, crystalline strychnine.

Once, visiting Yaddo, I met Hope Davis, wife of the critic Robert Gorham Davis. A writer for a ladies' magazine which often printed sentimental verse, Davis did not credit herself with much critical insight. Besides, she had recently visited Frost and seemed to accept the benign self-image he marketed. When I read her this poem, however, she looked up, shocked: "Why, that's what adults do to children!"

This is one of the poems, then, that reflects the death of Frost's first child—treated most directly in "Home Burial." In 1900, hoping for more time to write, Frost had left a teaching position and moved his family to a farm near Methuen, Massachusetts. That winter, his three-year-old son, Elliott, contracted cholera and died. Frost later said that his wife had blamed their move for the child's death and used it to turn the rest of the family against him. Rightly or not, he obviously felt much guilt, as may be seen in such related poems as "In Hardwood Groves" or "A Leaf Treader."

Here, the imaging of the child as one of those pools that "reflect / The total sky almost without defect" is made more physically explicit by echoes of Andrew Marvell's "On a Drop of Dew," where the newborn soul

> . . . the clear region where 'twas born,
> Round in itself incloses.

Many will also hear echoes of Wordsworth's child "trailing clouds of glory . . . / From God, who is our home." The poem, then, is almost a conceit: the pond represents the child; the "dark foliage," the "leaves" of Frost's books; the ravenous trees, the poet himself. "How little good my health has done," he said after the suicide of another son, Carol, "for anyone dear to me!"

Frost's "Out, Out," closely related, though directly based on the accidental death of a neighbor child, is no less controlled by juxtaposed but covert images—even more strongly visual and abetted by biblical and literary allusions.

OUT, OUT

> The buzz saw snarled and rattled in the yard
> And made dust and dropped stove-length sticks of wood,
> Sweet-scented stuff when the breeze drew across it.
> And from there those that lifted eyes could count
> Five mountain ranges one behind the other
> Under the sunset far into Vermont.
> And the saw snarled and rattled, snarled and rattled,
> As it ran light, or had to bear a load.

And nothing happened: day was all but done.
Call it a day, I wish they might have said
To please the boy by giving him the half hour
That a boy counts so much when saved from work.
His sister stood beside them in her apron
To tell them "Supper." At the word, the saw,
As if to prove saws knew what supper meant,
Leaped out at the boy's hand, or seemed to leap—
He must have given the hand. However it was,
Neither refused the meeting. But the hand!
The boy's first outcry was a rueful laugh,
As he swung toward them holding up the hand
Half in appeal, but half as if to keep
The life from spilling. Then the boy saw all—
Since he was old enough to know, big boy
Doing a man's work, though a child at heart—
He saw all spoiled. "Don't let him cut my hand off—
The doctor, when he comes. Don't let him sister!"
So. But the hand was gone already.
The doctor put him in the dark of ether.
He lay and puffed his lips out with his breath.
And then—the watcher at his pulse took fright.
No one believed. They listened at his heart.
Little—less—nothing!—and that ended it.
No more to build on there. And they, since they
Were not the one dead, turned to their affairs.

From the first, the saw is menacing, half-alive—its purpose,
seemingly, not to cut firewood but to make dust, the stuff of death.
That is countered, though, by a surprisingly beautiful vision:

And from there those that lifted eyes could count
Five mountain ranges one behind the other
Under the sunset far into Vermont.

The sense of echoing distance is enhanced by reverberant
sounds: "count . . . mountain . . . other / Under . . . far . . . Vermont."

And we have a reassuring biblical echo: "I will lift up mine eyes unto the hills whence cometh my salvation."

Still, around heavy machinery, it's better not to lift your eyes. The boy lifts his—not to count ranges, perhaps, but to count time "saved from work." A fearful salvation is granted: not a half hour but a lifetime saved from work. Lifting *our* view from saw to horizon reveals a terrifying analogy: we are given one glimpse, ironically lovely, of the jagged teeth of a world ready to take us for *its* "Supper."

If we had wondered why there should be five ranges—neither four nor six—there's a certain aptness to the "meeting" of saw and hand: five ranges, five fingers. This is the hand with which the boy had worked, cutting—figuratively devouring—the wood which would warm both him and his supper. It is as if the two shook hands—say, before combat—but the first touch destroys the boy. The sunset, at first so beautiful, takes on an implicit horror as the teeth of that world-saw redden. Yet the beauty is real, too—just as we found the saw's work unexpectably lovely: "Sweet-scented stuff when the breeze drew across it." Beauty, as always for Frost, is dangerous—like the woods, "lovely, dark and deep." Ever to lift your eyes from work, from the promises you've made, can cost you. Yet even the moment of the kill may have beauties—especially for those who don't happen to be "the one dead."

For its superscription, "Out, Out" might take the old hymn, "Work for the night is coming when man works no more." In Freud's world, only work and love could give life meaning; in Frost's, it's just half that. The image of world as buzz saw looms over the whole poem. The boy's sister wears an apron, the uniform of her work; the boy recognizes death in the word he'd have spoken about a mis-sawn board: "spoiled." (Reinforced by sound echoes, "spilling . . . child . . . spoiled," the word offers many implications.) Finally, the little group of watchers realizes that there's "No more to build on there." Their society, the texture and structure of communal life, is like house construction or cabinet work: pieces are shaped, then joined for mutual reinforcement. Like bungled carpentry, the boy is past attachment or relationship; he can only be discarded.

As the night of unworking draws on, the earlier biblical echo, "those that lifted eyes," yields to a new cluster of images: The boy's family, his neighbors, finally all of us are seen as like a city under siege. The watcher at the boy's pulse recalls the "watchman at the gate," looking not upward for salvation, but open-eyed against inevitable invasion. The boy's eyes are—after one glimpse of the "all"—delivered by a more merciful dark. Others, unless and until they become "the one dead," can only turn to their affairs, their work.

Necessary though that may be, the poem's ending still has some sense of guilt, some suggestion that "they" should have been more deeply grieved. This was foreshadowed in the sweet scent of the sawdust (a pleasure derived from the saw's work) and in the speculation that the boy "must have given the hand"—as if that could mitigate an implied accusation. In "Home Burial," the indictment unuttered in "Out, Out" is spoken by the neurotically blameful wife, fiercely denying that she feels anything but unadulterated grief for her child's death:

> If you had any feelings, you that dug
> With your own hands—how could you?—his little grave; . . .
> You could sit there with the stains on your shoes
> Of the fresh earth from your own baby's grave
> And talk about your everyday concerns . . .
> You *couldn't* care . . .
> Friends make pretense of following to the grave,
> But before one is in it, their minds are turned
> And making the best of their way back to life . . .
> But the world's evil . . .

Just so, the speaker of "A Leaf Treader" charges himself with refusing the falling leaves' "invitation to grief" and of triumphantly trampling them under: "Now up my knee to keep on top of another year of snow." Both poems assume that one's inescapable relief at not being "the one dead" implies a callous rapacity.

In contrast, we might turn to a figure who looked steadily at the world's horror, shook hands with the buzz saw and, though destroyed, triumphed. Many readers, Samuel Taylor Coleridge not least, have been haunted by a stanza from the ballad of "Sir Patrick Spens":

> Late, late yestreen I saw the new moone
> Wi' the auld moone in hir arme;
> And I feir, I feir, my master deir,
> That we will come to harme.

Spoken by one of Sir Patrick's crew just before their ship embarks on its ill-fated errand, the lines evoke both foreboding, grief, and a dimly perceived consolation for either a past or an expected loss. Some find it heavily redolent of a Pietà—fitting, because Sir Patrick and his men are, in a sense, sacrifices to their king's arrogant ignorance of his realm's weather.

Yet if that image of the moon is powerful in itself, it is even more important in tempering and unifying the whole ballad:

SIR PATRICK SPENS

> The king sits in Dumfermlin toune,
>   A-drinking the blude-reid wine:
> "Whar will I get me a skeely sailor
>   To sail this schip of mine?"
>
> Up and spak an eldern knicht,
>   Sat at the king's richt knee:
> "Sir Patrick Spens is the best sailor
>   That sails upon the se."
>
> The king has written a braid letter,
>   And signd it wi' his ain hand;
> And sent it tae Sir Patrick Spens,
>   Was walking on the sand.
>
> The first line that Sir Patrick red,
>   A loud lauch lauchèd he;

The next line that Sir Patrick red,
　The teir blinded his ee.

"O wha is this has don this deid,
　This ill deid don tae me;
Tae send me oot this time o' the yeir
　Tae sail upon the se?"

"Mak haste, mak haste, my mirry men all,
　Our guid schip sails the morne."
"O say na sae, my master deir,
　For I feir a deadlie storme.

"Late, late yestreen I saw the new moone
　Wi' the auld moone in hir arme;
And I feir, I feir, my master deir,
　That we will cum tae harme."

O our Scots nobles wer richt laith
　Tae weet their cork-heild shoone;
Bot lang owre a' the play wer playd,
　Thair hats they swam aboone.

O it's mony and mony a fedderbed
　Went flutterin tae the faem
And it's mony and mony a Scot laird's son
　Will nevir mair cam hame.

O lang, lang, may thair ladies sit
　Wi' their fans into thair hand,
Or eir they se Sir Patrick Spens
　Cum sailin tae the land.

O lang, lang, may thair ladies stand
　Wi' thair gold kems in their hair,
Waitin for thair ain deir lairds,
　Bot they'll se thame nae mair.

> Haf owre, haf owre to Aberdour
>   It's fiftie fadom deip,
> And thair lies guid Sir Patrick Spens,
>   Wi' the Scot lairds at his feit.

The singer (probably barefoot most of his life) openly scorns the Scottish nobles mincing along lest they soil their fancy, cork-heeled French pumps, mocks the young lords drowning among their featherbeds and luxuries, the grieving wives with their costly fans and combs. Yet for all its envious mockery, that image of the ladies' combs takes a curious resonance from the earlier image of the "new moone with the auld moone in her arme." In the first image we saw a blanked-out circle enclosed on one edge by a ring of shining light. The later image is strikingly similar: an ill-defined, even waxen, head and face edged by a bright ring of gold.

Because of this likeness of gold comb to crown, of the new moon to a "corona," the resonance of that image reaches to both ends of the ballad. In the first stanza we saw the king himself, careless of wind or tide in the world he rules, carousing with his court. There he towered over that "eldern knicht" who sat not at his right hand or elbow but at his knee. In the last stanza, we see Sir Patrick lying at the bottom of the sea "wi the Scot lairds at his feit." He, who knew too well the probable cost yet set out upon his duty, thus assumes the king's place among the dead.

Nothing is harder than to compose a poem or song about someone who does things right. "Sir Patrick Spens," at least partly because of its scorn for the ignorant royal court, seems superbly successful in recognizing a more genuine nobility. Not that I need agree with its values: personally, I'd prefer (though scarcely expect) a captain with more loyalty to his men than to king and office. Yet while the song lasts, I partake of the Scottish singer's world and so am broadened by access to another's experience and values. The images of new moon and of gold comb, both so effective in themselves, contribute heavily not only to the structure of the whole but to the ballad's deepest question: who, under the aspect of eternity, shall wear the crown?

III.

When a grasp of both objects being compared is so crucial, one might ask why one of those objects can or should remain merely implicit. Why should a poem or song make such demands on our wits? In "Sir Patrick Spens," the reason seems obvious: personal safety. Open criticism of one's rulers is seldom conducive to long life: the German public's ignorance of what happened to the Jews, the American public's ignorance of matters in Central and South America, suggest we don't dare know some of the things we can't help knowing. When ignorance offers affluence or power, even survival, it may be folly to air one's unconscious.

Art's mission *is* to reveal; *what* it reveals, however, is not some objective truth about the world's conditions, but rather the nature of the mind experiencing that world—the nature, if you like, of cerebral response. If psychoanalysis has taught us one thing, it's that much within the brain is held only in encoded forms. To pretend that such material is readily accessible would mean not only distorting the responses art records but, worse, pretending to superiorities which, in our case, we have not got.

The mind's disguises—its lies, evasions, concealings—may tell us as much as does the matter disguised. It seems probable that such material may be excluded from the left hemisphere's verbal and analytic command, and taken instead into the right hemisphere with its emphasis not only on music but on space and shape. Recalling the right hemisphere's predilection for puns, we might note that the comparisons we've been discussing are a kind of visual pun—substituting for what is hidden not a similar sound but a similar shape. One more way a work of art may reveal what the mind does not know it knows.

There are, of course, threats beyond physical danger—threats to one's theories about the world or about oneself, threats of mental or emotional pain. To have seen, too clearly, the beast's "naked foot" lurking within the lady's might have forced Wyatt either to forgo that "once, in special" she offered him or now to forgo blaming her because he had overestimated her intentions or his ability to influence them.

We give lesser credence to those who talk too readily about such matters as their child's death, about the fear they may, in part, have caused that death or might then have felt anything but unallayed grief. We might suspect that the artist's motive may not be to render alive and experienceable such a snarl of thoughts and feelings, but rather to flaunt their analytic powers or their excellence in confessing faults.

Describing what is really the same motive and its methods, one of my old professors, Victor Harris, said: "The secret of being perfectly dull is to answer all the questions." To ensure against any such perfection, I will turn to a poem that raises far more questions than I would even try to answer – one of the century's most moving love poems, which we are lucky to have in one of our finest translations.

SIX YEARS LATER
—Joseph Brodsky, trans. Richard Wilbur

So long had life together been that now
The second of January fell again
On Tuesday, making her astonished brow
Lift like a windshield-wiper in the rain,
   So that her misty sadness cleared, and showed
   A cloudless distance waiting up the road.

So long had life together been that once
The snow began to fall, it seemed unending;
That, lest the flakes should make her eyelids wince,
I'd shield them with my hand, and they, pretending
   Not to believe that cherishing of eyes
   Would beat against my palm like butterflies.

So alien had all novelty become
That sleep's entanglements would put to shame
Whatever depths the analysts might plumb;
That when my lips blew out the candle-flame,

Her lips, fluttering from my shoulder, sought
To join my own, without another thought.

So long had life together been, that all
That tattered brood of papered roses went,
And a whole birch-grove grew upon the wall,
And we had money, by some accident,
   And tonguelike on the sea, for thirty days,
   The sunset threatened Turkey with its blaze.

So long had life together been without
Books, chairs, utensils—only that ancient bed,
That the triangle, before it came about,
Had been a perpendicular, the head
   Of some acquaintance hovering above
   Two points which had been coalesced by love.

So long had life together been that she
And I, with our joint shadows, had composed
A double door, a door which even if we
Were lost in work or sleep, was always closed:
   Somehow, it would appear, we drifted right
   On through it into the future, into the night.

Pleased that their anniversary falls on its original weekday, the couple can hope the woman's "misty sadness" may lift. As her eyebrows arch with pleasure, both see, as through the curved spaces on a windshield, the rain clearing and a "cloudless distance" ahead. Yet snow comes on; as "he" tries to shield "her" eyes, the wipers' sweeping turns, first, to the beating of her lashes, then of butterflies' wings—a remembrance of summer and romance. Tender as that image is, though, we know the butterflies—like the woman's eyes—are trying to escape.

This image of wings is transferred, next, from the woman's eyes to her lips, apparently wanting only to join the man's. Yet as he blows out the candle, before they make love, night (bringing that love's and the poem's end) is falling. Knowing about moths and candles, we understand, however covertly, that some attraction has been extinguished. True, in the fourth stanza, the couple's joined lips seem to bring a new and more hopeful vista which, unframed by any windshield's shape or chilling snow, fills their field of vision. The familiar surroundings are replaced by "a whole birch grove [growing] upon the wall," the quenched candle by an exotic and passionate sunset's blaze. Yet, with its strange tongue, that sunset (like Frost's) is ominous; even the boast of its duration—all of thirty days—only underlines its brevity.

If the fourth stanza seems to release us from recurrent and confining shapes, the fifth, which presents the infidelity, renews those figures' force. As material items are stripped away from the couple and the third lover appears merely as "some acquaintance," personal attributes are lost; the relationship takes the rigid, almost mechanical figure of a triangle. This seemingly novel image actually angulates the earlier pattern of windshield-eyes-butterflies. Like the wiper, this latest geometrical figure started as a perpendicular; its hinged action creates the triangle, thus spreading and parting the lovers, the two points once "coalesced by love." The flames that earlier had threatened Turkey have now spread.

The last stanza carries out a final transformation of this pattern of shapes. The lovers become a double door seen from above—just as the "acquaintance" had seen them. This pair of swinging doors mimics the movement of the windshield wipers—and of the eyes which would not believe their partner's cherishing. Now, through these doors of their own vision, the lovers are vaulted as if through their own windshield into the emptiness of the night ahead.

So elaborate a construct of images might seem ill-suited, too mechanical or willed for a poem of direct personal feeling. Still, a subject so freighted with emotion may need this formalization, this stiffening against self-display. Again, the poet might well have been less than conscious of the patterns he was creating, striking upon a configuration so inherent to his thought that it might be recalled in any effort to speak of matters so painfully intimate.

It seems to me, however, that none of this poem's concrete and explicit images—wiper, butterfly, perpendicular and triangle, double doors—is ultimately basal; I suspect that some figure, revenant yet only immanent, underlies all these, taking each as a momentary embodiment—dare I say incarnation? My first thought is that this encompassing image is in some way genital—fitting for a poem about a lost love. Yet, on further thought, it seems that a deeper, more archtypal image lies beneath—that of a face. At least for myself, the two clearings on the windshield are shaped like and share the function of eyes; the wiper, like the perpendicular, may suggest a nose; the movement of the vertical line opens this into wings, then nostrils, and at last into swinging doors. And we do not need the example of modern artists to show that images of face and genitals may superimpose—we have Mona Van Duyn's oyster and smilebutton.

Finally, I am reminded that a crying baby will sometimes be comforted—may stop crying—if you draw for it a cartoon of a pair of eyes: the image of the mother's eyes, which mean it will soon be fed. As the baby grows older, you add a mouth, then a nose, and so forth. These are almost the first visual impressions upon a baby's developing mind; to go earlier, we must revert to the burst of light at the moment of birth or to sounds and rhythms known in the womb. It is scarcely surprising that such an image should underlie much that we might see later, particularly in moments of great emotion, moments when we might lose, once more, a face deeply loved.

Whether or not one cares to accept such speculations, it's clear that images such as those we've been considering, each a sort of "gray eminence" that governs the finished work, often reach far beneath any conscious intention of the poet and may be one of the surest signs of creative genius. We should not imagine such strokes of invention necessarily come as unsought, spontaneous gifts. Wordsworth's longer first version of "She Dwelt Among the Untrodden Ways," for instance, contained nearly all the material now in that tiny masterpiece; there, however, it was not only spoiled by poor rhythms and silly phrasing but was surrounded by so much trite filler that it could not be recognized. Art imitates life in this, too: it may be born corrupted but, with luck and skillful management, grow toward integrity.

Again, so rich a construct of less-than-conscious images and ideas as appears in "Sir Patrick Spens" may seem improbable in a poem of communal origin. Such unities could only rise, one might suppose, from deep within some remarkable personality, some sharply individuated self. Yet, as we must sadly remind ourselves, the individual, once freed from the limitations of the communal group, all too often refuses such richness of cortical involvement in favor of easy opinions or fashionable "causes," the proprieties of one's own faction. Those with a folkish ax to grind will, perhaps, take the rich gestalt of such a poem to prove the existence of a "folk soul." For me, it bespeaks the baffling unpredictability of the human psyche—that its brilliances, so often lacking when we need them, still arise at times when we might not have dared ask.

DISGRACING ARE VERSE:
SENSE, CENSORS, NONSENSE AND
EXTRASENSORY DECEPTION

I. Codes, Hums and Puns

"Wants pawn term, dare worsted ladle gull hoe lift wetter murder inner ladle cordage honor itch offer lodge dock florist. Disc ladle gull orphan worry ladle cluck wetter putty rat hut, end fur disc raisin, pimple colder ladle rat rotten hut."

Who has so debauched our bedtime story? Everything's encoded into sounds we must decipher and reconstitute! Once we recognize, under this weird linguistic getup, our heroine's little cloak and pretty red hood, we—like the "wicket woof" himself—are likely to exclaim, "Wail, wail, wail . . . evanescent ladle rat rotten hut!"

Still, why crack our shins on such a verbal obstacle course? Why trail this phonetically corrupted child with her "burden barter and shirker car keys" through a "dock florist" of puns and echoes to her "groinmurder's cordage." We'll only find the "curl and bloat Thursday woof" is there already, wearing "err groinmurder's nut cup and gnat gun . . . curdle dope inner bet" and "disgracing is verse." And, while the child questions his disguise, why should *we* be trying to penetrate *her* linguistic camouflage? "O Grammar . . . Wart bag icy gut! A nervous sausage bag ice! . . . O Grammar, water bag noise! A nervous sore suture anomalous prognosis! . . . O Grammar, water bag mousey gut! A nervous sore suture bag mouse!" Finally, once the "woof" has "ceased pore ladle rat rotten hut and garbled erupt," what makes us whoop with delight at that stern cautionary moral: "Yonder nor sorghum stenches shut ladle gulls stopper torque wet strainers"?

Such diversions are truly addictive; soon we too sound like refugees from some Balkan revolution: "Dent stopper torque wet strainers." "Hoe cake, murder!" We write letters in Graustarkian dialects, spend weeks decoding our friends' replies. Are we out of our minds? If not, where in our minds *are* such dialects spoken?

77

The language of *Ladle Rat Rotten Hut*— the "Anguish Languish"—was devised by Professor Howard Chace for the disorientation of folk tales. As children, we too invented dialects for use with friends. "Latins," we called them—implying an erudition which, in our case, we had not got. In medieval Provence, the vernaculars which were becoming our modern Romance languages were called "Latis" (i.e., "Latins") in honor of that tongue they were driving out. At our young age, though, we knew nothing of Latis or of Latin itself. Even English sometimes sounded foreign; why make up newer, more difficult languages?

Like most kids, we started with pig Latin:

Ellway, it'say ikelay isthay . . .

But since everyone knew that, we invented V Latin:

Wevell, ivit's livike thivis. . . .

and when too many got the knack of that, egg Latin:

Weggell, eggit's leggike theggis . . .

Chris Evert, the tennis star, reported that her childhood circle added "ong" to every syllable:

Wongell, ongit's longike thongis . . .

which must have sounded like a gamelan orchestra.

My Mexican-American sister-in-law and her sister excluded their younger siblings by inserting "ethag" into every syllable; for syllables beginning with a vowel, "thag" was used:

Wethagel, ithagit's lethagike thethagis . . .

She still can speak this tongue faster than English; her son at age five could instantly grasp it without instruction. The code's use in family warfare reminds me that my younger sister, if detected in some misconduct, always claimed, with firm conviction: "Bobie Dobie did it!" That villainous cognomen must have been an amalgam of her older sister's name, Barbara, or Babs, with my nickname, De.

A few years ago, we enjoyed the stories Victor Borge punctuated with oral clicks, spurts and mouthed sounds, or the "inflationary language" in which he told of a Lieut-elevenant on the Police Fivce who was trying three fiveget something he nine. French students have a freer sort of pig Latin called "Verlan," a name derived by Verlanning the word "l'inverse," meaning "inside out" or "upside down." The gang of boys in *A Clockwork Orange* spoke a Russian-based slanguage, "Nadsat." In Cockney rhyming Latin, a man's wife is his storm and strife; some words are spelled backwards—a boyo becomes a yobbo – so involving the order of letters rather than sounds, exchanging aural for visual thought functions.

Children love rebuses, puzzles where some words are replaced by pictures of objects with like-sounding names. For "I," you get a drawing of an eye; for "dear," a deer. Like the Cockney Latin, rebuses have an added hurdle: a leap from the pictorial to the verbal, which may explain why their verbal play is usually pretty mild. We seldom get anything so comically far-fetched as "sorghum stenches" for "circumstances" or "evanescent" for "if it isn't."

More sophisticated rebuses are found in Susan Boynton's cartoons for greeting cards and wrapping paper. Her Yuletide giftwrap displays two lines of cartooned animals: the first line has a minnow, a sheep, a horse, several long-necked birds, then a moose; the label above them reads, "Wee fish, ewe, a mare, egrets, moose." The second line has a panda bear, a hippopotamus, a large horned beast and a reindeer; their label: "Panda, hippo, gnu, deer." In puzzles so strenuous, the animals' names must be supplied lest any buyers be excluded for lack of wit or enterprise.

In our schoolboy Latins, exclusion was all. We yearned to be insiders, in the know, protected by membership. That entailed a less innocent pleasure: someone had to be outside, yearning to get in. And admittedly, exclusion has often added to the pleasures of poetry. Going back through anthologies published between, say, 1850 and 1930, one is embarrassed by all the dialect tales and poems meant to mock minorities—German, Jewish, Irish, Italians, Blacks. Some seem less offensive:

BALLAD OF THE MERMAID
—Charles Godfrey Leland

Der noble Ritter Hugo
  Von Schwillensaufenstein,
Rode out mit shpeer und helmet,
  Und he coom to de panks of de Rhine.

And oop dere rose a meermaid
  Vot hadn't got nodings on,
Und she say, "Oh, Ritter Hugo,
  Vhere you goes mit yourself alone?"

Hearing that he rides through "de creenwood" to "ein Gasthaus" where he "trinks some peer," the "meermaid" displays her full range of temptations:

"Shoost look at dese shpoons and vatchess!
  Shoost see dese diamant rings!
Coom down und fill your bockets,
  Und I'll giss you like every dings. . . .

Dat fetched him—he shtood all shpell-pound
  She pooled his coat-tails down,
She drawed him oonder der wasser,
  De maiden mit nodings on.

Most examples, though, are too poor even to quote, except when their sniggerings occasionally backfire. Here, a Black preacher refers to St. Paul's Epistle to the Ephesians:

I like fo' to read 'bout the blessed Holy Ghos'
  An' de saints an' de mahacles and veesions,

> But de part ob de Book dat I liked de mos'
> Is where Paul p'ints his 'pistle at the 'Phesians.

Perhaps the editors of smarmy collections like *Heart Throbs* did not know the slang term for penis. Whatever *he* knew, the poem brings little credit to its author, Nixon Waterman. Better he had given us an eighteen-minute gap.

Not even William Shakespeare was proof against such bathroom (or outhouse) humor. In *Twelfth Night*, Malvolio questions a letter supposedly from his mistress, Olivia:

> By my life, this is my lady's hand. These be her very c's,
> her n's, and her t's, and thus makes she her great P's.

In *Cymbeline*, Cloten tries to seduce Imogen by leading some musicians to her door:

> I am advis'd to give her music a' mornings; they say
> it will penetrate. Come on; tune; if you can penetrate
> her with your fingering, so; we'll try with tongue
> too.

If we can't *always* admire the Bard's inclusiveness, at least we know whether the character or the author is shown to be a booby.

After the genocidal horrors and the racial upheavals of the last century, dialect verse has grown unfashionable. Not that we are less prejudiced (or even less genocidal); we *are* less willing to display that in public. Such clannish snobbery is usually banished to the demimonde of the ethnic joke. Some of that patronizing superiority, more affectionately tinted, appears in our amusement at children's unconscious parodies of public ceremonies like those gathered by William Safire. Here again, we find phrases that recall revered texts but yield comical images:

> I led the pigeons to the flag . . .
> and to the republic for Richard Stans,
> one naked individual . . .

or even

one nation, on a bicycle . . .

Teachers too collect students' attempts at quotation: "O Wind, if Winter comes, can Spring be bare behind?"
 Meantime, we try to forget our own childhood hymnodies:

Red and yellow, black and blue,
They are precious in his sight,
For He loves the little children of the world.

or

Away in a manger, no crib for a bed,
The little Lord Jesus laid down his soft head . . .

Small wonder that during our induction rites into adulthood—rites which could make sense only after years of vigorous brainwashing—we often mistranslated. Not all our parodies, of course, were unconscious:

We three kings of Orient are,
Smoking on a rubber cigar.
It was loaded, and kasploded;
Now we're on yonder star.

 Mildly off-color jokes lurked on every side; we asserted that the "p" in "psalm" was silent—as in swimming. Some could transubstantiate a curse: "Cheese and crackers got all muddy!" The highly skilled could merge the words "Horse shit!" into a sneeze, leaving the adults outraged but uncertain. We invented book titles: *The Tiger's Revenge,* by Claude Balls, or *Spots on the Sheet* by Mister Completely. We recited long, pun-filled "routines" with titles like "The Midnight Handicap" or "Daniel in the Lion's Den," which concluded, "Thereupon, Daniel was called to come forth. But he slipped on a lion turd and came in fifth." Years later I recognized this as an element (with an added pun) from the funeral games in *The Iliad*. (Homer proves surprisingly ubiquitous: my upstate New York auto mechanic, who lived near a village named Homer, once unwittingly paraphrased Tiresias's directions for determining where to build your home, substituting snow tires for Odysseus's oar.)

Linguistic pranks surface even in adults. I knew an elderly lady, prim of mien, who if treated rudely by a clerk might reply, in her sweetest voice, "Well, fuck you very much" and walk demurely away. My urologist, who says he dislikes poetry, often sports a versified button:

> 2 P
> C Me

And adults still love parodies of their most beloved ceremonies. The more securely we believe in something, the more readily we can give play to inevitable doubts. A theatrical (and patriotic) colleague once smuggled a whole dramatic cast into "The Star Spangled Banner":

PRINCIPAL CHARACTERS IN THE NATIONAL ANTHEM

1. José Canusi—Mexican guitarist
2. Dawn Zerlilite—Baltimore stripper
3. Fatso Proudly—Stand-up comedian
4. Lee Streaming—Minneapolis attorney
5. Whose Broad—Attractive amnesia victim
6. Perry Les Phyte—Advertising executive
7. Gallant Lee—2-yr. old gelding; winner, 1966 Preakness
8. Red Glare—Oriole's short stop, 1931–37
9. Orlando De Frie—Italian industrialist
10. Homo the Brave—Gay wrestler from Los Angeles

Not the least aim in such games is to defeat the censor through an unspecified and disguised mockery of whatever our society reveres. Who can forget the Crispness Carols:

Good King Sauerkraut, look down:
All your feet's uneven! . . .

or:

Deck us all with Boston, Charlie,
    Wall walla wash and Kalamazoo!
Nora's freezing on the trolley,
    Swaller dollar cauliflower
Alley-ga-roo

Sentimental songs are vulnerable not only to Pogo:

Wassail I do
Wenc'las is far away
And Moll Malone
Wass'l I do?

But also to Dave Morrah:

Darn body oat meal stream,
    Wear a fierce mate shoe,
Ouija eyesore blue
    Dresden kingdom dew,
Litmus dare anew
    Thatch aloft me too.
Ewer sex-steam,
Marvel itch Queen,
Darn bawdy oat meal scream!

Comparable is John Frederick Nims' alleged discovery of the poem "Therese" by Joe E. Skilmer: "*I* think??? *That* I shall never—see?"

Such pranks come natural to poets; their mission, after all, is to create language which means other—preferably more—than its everyday, dictionary denotation. For recreation, they mock not only artists they scorn, like Joyce Kilmer, but even—perhaps especially—those they admire. Kenneth Koch provided parodies of

William Carlos Williams, Robert Frost, even Shakespeare: "Tube heat or nog tube heat: data's congestion." At poets' parties, the favorite amusement has long been to render classics in improbable voices: W. C. Fields reciting "Lycidas," Groucho delivering "Prufrock"—or, as noted earlier, to sing great poems to outrageous melodies.

Others, too, (I almost wrote, "Adults, too") delight in such linguistic play. When *New York Magazine* held a competition for the invention of odd couples, the multitudinous entries included Hops and Ed Koch, Yassir and Syngman Rhee, Alice and Oy Faye. The best examples not only displayed wildly distorted spellings and pronunciations, they yoked the famous or respected with things low and disgraceful: No Pest and Meryl Streep, Great Ball and William Safire.

A few decades ago, elephant jokes gave us iconoclastic pleasures, soothing our irritation at the world's disproportions: the large were cut down, the small inflated; the sacrosanct brought low, the trivial made mighty. Elephants painted their toenails to hide in cherry trees; the leviathan shrank to Moby Grape. The 2,000-pound canary slept anywhere he liked and, down some midnight alley, belched a profundo, "Here, kitty, kitty, kitty." The once infallible pontiff became Pope Pickle; Octopus Rex limped about wearing black glasses. Film stars were transmogrified into Fred Asparagus and Lana Turnip.

Downgrading the revered and respected are, of course, delights native to *Ladle Rat Rotten Hut*. Despite her pretty clothes, our heroine is a "Rat" who holds unspecified traffickings with some "Rotten Hut." Grandmother, traditional font of familial benevolence, becomes "groinmurder," a veritable godperson of sex and violence. Her homely nightcap and nightgown are transmuted into a "nut cup and gnat gun" (the former a protective device worn by football players). The wolf not only ate the child, he "garbled erupt," compounding fraud with belchlike grossness. The story itself has been outrageously fudged: our heroine bridles at the wolf's facial features, " O Grammar . . . a nervous sausage anomalous prognosis." Beyond the absurdity of a jittery sausage, beyond the "noses" hidden inside "prognosis," it's implied that the poor child actually said, "I never saw such an abominable proboscis"—words utterable only by "Fats" Waller or Jimmy Durante.

In many puns and word games, aggression is turned not only against society's shibboleths but against the reader or listener. "Knock, knock" jokes are notably deceitful:

> Knock, knock.
> Who's there?
> Eskimos, Christians and Italians.
> Eskimos, Christians and Italians who?
> Eskimos Christians and Italians no lies!

We've been led to imagine a vast crowd of immigrants huddled on our doorstep then banished by a garbled folk adage. Similar deceptions lurk in "feghoots," wildly improbable shaggy-dog stories which end in just such scrambled names or proverbs: "The Moron Tab and Apple Choir" or "The son of the squaw on the hippopotamus equals the sons of the squaws on the other two hides." Such transpositions abound in the sayings attributed to the Reverend Dr. William A. Spooner of Oxford, who reputedly commiserated with his congregation's vague desires: "We all . . . have a half-warmed fish within us." As children, we got others to repeat and memorize a set of nonsense syllables:

> Awah (pause)
> Tahgoo (pause)
> Siam

then sing them to the tune of "My Country, 'Tis of Thee." William Arrowsmith, translator of Aristophanes' *The Knights*, presents two slaves, afraid even to voice the desire to flee their masters. One teaches the other to say, slowly, "Wallets, go 'way!" then to repeat this phrase faster and faster until it becomes "Let's go AWOL! Let's go AWOL!" Thus we not only release aggressions against the hearer and against our society; we also re-discover something of the pleasures a child takes in finding once-nonsensical sounds to have defined meanings.

Ladle Rat Rotten Hut must be one of our longest puns, a charade game whose answer must be guessed from what the clues "sound like." Or a variant on "Name That Tune"—we are given the "music" of a text, its phonology or sound, as a clue to the original words. Such an exercise is energetic and complicated, tickling one mental connection to fire off another old, half-forgotten one. Neurologists tell us that most of our handling of language, at least of semantics and syntax, is managed in the left hemisphere; music (except for rhythm) by the right. "Name That Tune," then, encompasses a wide brain span; re-creating a connection across hemispheres. Once again we are asking disparate areas of the mind and brain to refire an old pattern of synapses.

Reversing this process, as a student I made up inane lyrics to help recall pieces of classical music; certain standard symphonic works still insistently recall the gooey phrases I supplied for them. Tchaikovsky's Fourth still echoes Meredith Wilson's voice singing:

> In the field is standing a birch tree,
> In the field is standing a birch tree,
> Tra-la-la-la-la-la birch tree,
> Tra-la-la-la-la-la birch tree . . .

Thank God he never helped us remember Mozart!

Still, music can help us to rewire "forgotten" connections with the conscious language centers, so helping us express thoughts and feelings we've repressed as immoral or otherwise threatening. Tunes we half-consciously hum can provide interesting, often embarrassing, clues to our real thoughts. Sitting beside a lady, we may find we're singing, "I wish I were single again" or, worse, "Why do I love you?" Occasionally, I have first recognized how threatening I found some situation on noticing that I'd been humming an old Scots ballad of betrayal: "She was trantin' and dancin' and singin' for joy; / She's vowed that very night she would feast Inverey," i.e., the cattle thief who had just murdered her husband.

Music, then, can restore speech capacities and is specially helpful to patients whose language has been impaired by brain damage. Such patients are first retaught the "music" of language, starting with phonology and rhythms, so encouraging unimpaired areas of the brain to take over the management of language. We often teach foreign languages the same way: letting students learn first, as a baby does, the music of the language, then imposing semantics and syntax upon that.

There is a priority, probably related, in the physiology of language-making: we create the rhythm of speech first. The voice originates as a series of puffs and pulses, a stream of air created by the diaphragm well before the lips and vocal folds impart the vowels and consonants which give rise to semantics and syntax. Which again calls up T. S. Eliot's statement—corroborated by William Butler Yeats, Virginia Woolf and Paul Valéry, among others—that a poem might announce itself first as a rhythm before finding words.

Most readers would admit a like process in reading and appreciation. We often think: "I don't know what this poem means, but it's marvelous and I *will* know, *could* know if I wanted." I read many favorites this way: Theodore Roethke's "Lost Son" poems, many of John Berryman's "Dream Songs," Robert Lowell's early poems. Of course, we dare not dismiss, unexplored, the poem's conscious sense; yet we simply don't "understand" Hart Crane or Dylan Thomas as we do a set of instructions. Such poets create, as Dr. Johnson said of John Milton, a "Babylonish dialect." Is not the "music" of such poems at least as important as their message content? And as that "music" becomes increasingly prominent, doesn't it lift the poem farther from its "sense"—even as, should we restore the poem to its ancient condition of song, we may almost remove it from the realm of conscious meaning? To borrow Karl Shapiro's term, may not the words, as they take on more music, become "not-words," become nonsense, not-sense, new-sense? And don't the literal-minded always find "new-sense" to be a nuisance?

Ezra Pound, who surely had one of our finest poetic ears, advised young poets to listen to poetry in languages they don't understand. If I have some notion of the general situation, I actually like plays performed in languages strange to me. I may rent one of those simultaneous pocket translators but only use it long enough to know, "Oh yes, this is Medea's big speech where she tells Jason he can. . . ." Then I want to drop the sense of individual words and phrases, catching instead the rise and fall, the surge and ebb of emotion in the actor's voice.

Indeed, I once found I understood one play better in a language I didn't know. Not long after seeing *Barefoot in the Park* in New York, I saw it in Budapest. In the absence of the jokery that covers its surface like filigree on inferior silver, I got the meaning of the underlying action. It became clear why the playwright situates his newlyweds in a seven-story walk-up—they always pant heavily on entrance; why the young groom always removes his necktie to press inside a book; why toes are constantly dabbled in the hearth rug's fur; why, when the pair quarrels, the phone cord is yanked out of its socket; why the angry groom crawls out the window and might fall off the roof. We're being shown, by agencies of plot and imagery, that if the male accepts certain anatomical and functional alterations, the marriage and the play may end happily; when we were distracted by gags and patter, that message stayed below the conscious level.

Operagoers, of course, have long listened to dramas in other languages. Both musical and literary works can benefit from associations with the other form. We have already noted how a musical phrase may entail a set of words—just as a set of words can call up a melody. In Thomas Hardy's *The Mayor of Casterbridge*, the heroine compares herself to her wealthy neighbor: "What was she beside Lucetta?—as one of the 'meaner beauties of the night, when the moon had risen in the skies,'" so recalling an exquisite madrigal by Michael East and bringing into the plainer world of Casterbridge and Mellstock an air of Elizabethan romance and elegance.

Allusions to and quotations from songs are, of course, frequent in Shakespeare—most pointedly when they reveal thoughts that must be disguised even from the character—so underlining once again the ties between music and the unconscious. This is most obvious, perhaps, in the mad Ophelia's songs:

> Quoth she, before you tumbled me,
> You promised me to wed.

He answers:

> So would I ha' done, by yonder sun,
> An thou hadst not come to my bed.

The song reveals a sense of deepest personal betrayal which neither her character nor her situation would permit direct utterance.

Such quotations and "carrier" melodies can be just as useful to composers. John Dowland, in "Can She Excuse My Wrongs," has the lover, irked by his lady's chastity, ask himself—in a monotonous melodic line—a typical, self-pitying complaint:

> Wilt thou be thus abused still,
> Seeing that she will right thee never?
> If thou can'st not o'ercome her will
> Thy love will be thus fruitless ever.

Meantime, the accompaniment expresses his more vengeful (and musically livelier) thoughts, quoting a popular melody in the same rhythm: "Shall I go walk the woods so wild?" Even while the singer passively voices the lover's discontents, the wordless, "purer" music of the lute suggests more direct action: resorting to the nubile, willing females he imagines roaming the spring woods.

Yet we might remember our own experience of those woods. No doubt we too went there seeking other, lustier loves—believing ourselves wolves. We may have looked to others more like a little girl taking sugar cookies to her grandmother and were soon attacked by some "wicket woof" with his dialects, puns and knock-knocks. Such assaults do have compensations: even the lowest form of verbal aggression, the pun, can entertain its victim. Outwitted by some knocker at our mind's gates, we can share his (or her) triumph if we at least grasp the ingenuity that outmaneuvered us. We have peered through the disguise and the real meaning has not devoured us; garble has erupted, but we have survived. Our snark, neither a woof nor a boojum, has set us back on the right path through the woods, off to groinmurder's, chortling with glee.

We're like children who get tickled: a formation of unidentified words appeared; attack seemed imminent. Yet we're unhurt; the child laughs, triumphing over the threat. Many adults re-create over and over, to prove they can survive it, some injury they may (or may not) have suffered as a child. Isn't it a surer recreation to get tickled, to peer down the barrel of a pun? Puns (even those so long-barreled as *Ladle Rat Rotten Hut*) are always loaded—and sometimes go off. If they pepper us with confetti and shoot out a red flag (or even Rat Flack), haven't we a right to laugh? *Hoopla! Wir leben!*

II. The High Art of Mistranslation

Some years ago an anthology of recent American poems, newly translated into Romanian, appeared in Bucharest. As I happened to be there, I was invited to take part in a "spectacul," a staged poetry reading to celebrate this publication. I had to read not only my poems, but those of poets whose work I disliked and who, I knew, disliked mine. To play down such antagonisms, I tried to read everything energetically and vividly. After each poem, its new translation was read by a Romanian actor whose style was so deadpan that listeners must have doubted any relation could exist between the two texts.

This "spectacul" began with an academic lecture on the history of American poetry, starting with American Indian chants and Negro spirituals. One of these had a refrain which, during the several rehearsals, the lecturer read with great intensity:

O Maria, nu plinge, nu cîrîi.
O Maria, nu plinge, nu cîrîi.

Everyone found this lament deeply moving. Still, I had an uneasy sense of "echo"—shouldn't I know this song? Only during the actual performance before a live audience—it, too, moved by the reading—did the spiritual spring fullblown into my head:

> Oh, Mary, don't ya weep and don't ya moan;
> Oh, Mary, don't ya weep and don't ya moan.
>> Pharaoh's army got drownded;
>> Oh, Mary, don't ya weep!

Lament?—This is a shout of triumph at the destruction of one's enemies, usually sung by the whole congregation and accompanied by all available instruments, by hand-clapping, foot-stomping and parades through the church aisles. It was hard not to break into hilarity and spoil the moment's lyric solemnity.

With time, though, I've come to think the Romanian lecturer wasn't so far off the mark. After all, he didn't have the church setting, a Black congregation to sing, clap hands, play pianos or tambourines—the environmental orchestration was missing. No doubt he could have given a proper prose rendering—a Loeb Library translation:

> O Mary, cease your tears, desist from lamentation;
> The army of Pharaoh has been inundated.

Better to give us some experience, some emotion—a text true to some part of the often tragic history of Blacks in America.

Robert Frost wrote (paraphrasing Sir John Dunham) that "poetry is what evaporates in translation." Or drains off in embalming. Translators naturally hope to reinfuse the ichor of arteries formerly divine; ichor, alas, is in short supply. To avoid downright taxidermy, we must sometimes be content with mere human blood.

Anyone who doubts poetry's evaporability should consider M. D. Herter Norton's prose renderings of Rainer Maria Rilke. She provides a genuine service which may help English readers approach the German text—something like a map of a great city or guided tour through historic sights. To experience the full work of art you take up residence, learn the customs and habits of mind, inflections, the unspoken loyalties of that place. Mrs. Norton may leave you wondering why anyone thinks Rilke a poet at all. If, instead, a native speaker reads the original aloud, you'll not only know it's a poem, you may realize important aspects of its meaning structure. The last stanza of Rilke's early "Als du mich eins gefunden hast" runs:

> Da fühl ich, dass ich eines bin
> mit Mythe, Mai und Meer;
> und wie der Duft des Weines bin
> ich deiner Seele schwer.

Though I did not know German, when a friend read this to me I felt sure that the triple rhymes "eines bin" and "Weines bin" must enclose some pun or syntactic ambiguity. It does: the third line seems to be (like the first) a syntactic unit. The verb, "bin," however, runs over to become part of the fourth line—not ending the earlier clause but beginning the last. Such elegant linguistic play, with its rich music, seems at least as important as the prose sense.

In conversation, less than 10 percent of meaning is carried by message content; the rest lies in tone of voice, gesture, facial expression, bodily stance. In poems, where emotion runs so high, the percentage must be even more drastic. The poem says even less of what it means, may well convey its opposite: "Since that I so kindely am served . . ." or "humanity, i love you . . ." In the theatre we want actors not merely to deliver the denotational text, but to evince the embodied emotional subtext. In everyday life as well, we ask not only "What did he say?" but "What made him say that; what's he getting at?"

Using one of those pocket scores which highlights the leading melodic lines, I could probably sing through Beethoven's Third Symphony. Had I the voice of an angel, no listener would long endure the lack of harmony, orchestration, non-linear structure. A poem's "harmonization" and "orchestration" lie in what I have called "nonsense," "new-sense" or "near-sense": sound structures, alliterations, assonances, metrical and stanzaic forms, rhymes, levels and textures of language, strange and archaic words or coinages, references to other literary and linguistic forms (poems, songs, advertisements, etc.) Beyond that we have historic events unique to the culture, repetitions, invented or nonce syllables, refrains: *tra-la-la; derry derry down; with my glimpy, glimpy, eedle.* In short, elements that have little or no mandated meaning, whose meaning we must guess at, interpret—aspects of language which do the work of posture, facial expression and vocal inflection in daily conversation or of costume, ritual, procession and general mumbo jumbo in our public celebrations.

Shortly before my Romanian "spectacul," I visited the Writers' Union in Bulgaria. Asked what was happening in American poetry, I went back half a century to sketch the main movements and changes of our poetic atmosphere. After every few sentences, my remarks were translated by a young Bulgarian poet whose English was superb; he handled the material with astonishing ease. In his Bulgarian I heard every name I'd mentioned; later, questions from the group showed how completely he'd conveyed these complex and unfamiliar ideas.

Asked to read some of my own work, I picked a short piece, simple and fairly direct, the eighth from a cycle, "Heart's Needle." The poem, about pushing a child on a swing, implicitly compares that to the necessities of pushing her away, both in the normal process of growth and in the painful separations of divorce. At once, my translator became almost tongue-tied, stumbling over phrases, correcting or repeating himself, asking others for help, inserting parenthetical explanations. His hesitancy sprang not from any ineptitude, but directly from his grasp of, and responsibility to, the text. The simplest poem proved more resistant than the toughest critical prose.

I often say, half-joking, that it's easier to translate a poem if you don't know the original language. A bilingual translator almost unavoidably hears two versions simultaneously, one in each language; as these are stored separately by the brain, even the dullest translation yields a doubled excitation. Sadly, translations are not made for the bilingual. It is fraudulent to pretend that someone lacking the original language will find in a literal prose version either the stimulation felt by the bilingual (e.g., the translator) or by readers of the original.

If, living in New York, I had composed some music for violins, violas, cello and harp, I could no doubt sing its melodies over the phone for a friend in Los Angeles. It might be little use for him to know what my harp did in bar 33; he has an oboe, a bassoon, three trombones and some bongo drums. To interest hearers, he must exploit *his* instruments, his sense of harmony. Moving a poem to a second language will probably lose so many complex effects that I think it better to accept whatever richnesses the new language, the new orchestra, affords.

Years ago, Lore Segal and I translated together many of the comic poems of Christian Morgenstern. If I cite one here, it is to illustrate the dilemma, not to suggest that our solution was ideal. Where ideal solutions exist, there is no problem.

TAPETENBLUME

Tapetenblume bin ich fein,
kehr wieder ohne Ende,
doch, statt in Mai'n und Mondenschein,
auf jeder der vier Waende.

Du siehst mich nimmerdar genung,
so weit du blickst in Stuebchen,
und folgst du mir per Roesselsprung —
wirst du verrueckt, mein Liebchen.

A literal translation might run:

I am a fine wallpaper flower,
coming back again endlessly;
nonetheless, set in May and Moonshine
on all of the four walls.

You'll never see me enough
however far you look in the little room
and follow me by Knight's jumps [as in playing chess]
until you go insane, my darling.

Mildly amusing; one wouldn't go far to hear it. Losing music and shape, we lose the sense of literary tradition Morgenstern was parodying—those Romantic poems in which the flower, blooming each year in the May moonlight, stood for something of Essence, of eternal beauty. Trying to restore that movement, I've had to lengthen each stanza's second and fourth lines.

THE WALLPAPER FLOWER

I am a wallpaper flower, fine,
Renewed, returning endlessly.
But not in May and bright Moonshine;
On all four walls. You'll never see

Enough of me. You will pursue
Me round your little room, unspacious,
Bounding as Knights of the Chessboard do,
Till you go nuts, my precious.

Romantic tradition having grown unfamiliar, I've also underlined the mock-heroic with my "Knights of the Chessboard"—and, by a redoubled rhyme and runover stanza, emphasized the flower's relentless reappearance. Further, my last line is not only slangier than Morgenstern's; it tries to smuggle in an echo from *The Hobbit*. Immoral, perhaps, but necessary; so much is unavoidably lost from the original.

In translating one of Morgenstern's most charming poems, I give more rhymes than the original does:

PALMSTROEM AN EINE NACHTIGALL, DIE IHN NICHT SCHLAFEN LIESS

Moechtest du dich nicht in einen Fisch verwandeln
und gesanglich dementsprechend handeln?
dass sonst unmoeglich ist,
dass mir unternachts des Schlafes Labe
blueht, die ich nun doch notwendig habe!
    Tu es, wenn du edel bist!

Deine Frau im Nest wird dich auch so bewundern,
wenn du gaenzlich in der Art der Flundern
auftrittst und im Wipfel wohlig ruhst
oder, eine fliegende Makrele,
sie umflatterst, holde Philomele
  (—die du mir gewiss die Liebe tust!)

To rhyme, I've had to use nine shorter lines in place of Morgenstern's six. My rhymes, though more frequent, are often slanted and my lines less often end-stopped. I suspect that gives a different effect from that of the original—one I can only hope will satisfy a listener in English.

PALMSTROM TO A NIGHTINGALE
WHICH WOULD NOT LET HIM SLEEP

Why do you not transform
Yourself to a fish; and
In this matter of song, perform
Accordingly? For otherwise,
Through the long nights, how can
Slumber restore my eyes,
And blossom on my pillow,
Which is most needful? Then,
Do; if you are a noble fellow.

And your wife, too, on the nest —
How sweetly you will astound her
When you shine forth like a flounder
Blissfully at rest
On the top branch of your tree —
Or when you flutter around her
Like a flying mackerel,
Heavenly Philomel, —
You will do me this courtesy?

97

To change a poem or a song's rhythm, much less render it as free verse or prose, drastically alters its emotional tone and color, its relation to earlier works, its effect on a reader's expectations. Supposing Blake's "The Tyger" had ranged abroad not in trochees, but in iambs:

> O tyger, beast that burns so bright
> In darkling forests of the night,
> What godlike hand, what deathless eye
> Dare frame thy fearful symmetry?

The dire threat, the awestricken incantation vanish. In anapests, everything gets worse:

> O tyger, you creature that's burning so bright
> In threatening, gloom-shrouded forests of night,
> What hand of immortal, what deity's eye
> Dare hope it might frame thy most feared symmetry?

Or, if we *must* try triple metres, we might recall Aldous Huxley's revision of Milton's simile which found that Garden where Eve would soon be assaulted by Satan even lovelier than

> . . . that fair field
> Of Enna, where Prosperin gathring flours
> Her self a fairer Floure by gloomie Dis
> Was gatherd, which cost Ceres all that pain
> To seek her through the world; . . .

This, he revised *à la* Poe:

> It was noon in the fair field of Enna
>   Where Proserpina gathering flowers —
>   Herself the most fragrant of flowers,
> Was gathered away to Gehenna
>   By the Prince of Plutonian powers,
> Was borne down the windings of Brenner

To the gloom of his amorous bowers —
Down the torturous highway of Brenner
To the god's agapemonous bowers.

Yet, though a change of rhythm necessarily alters meaning, reproducing the original rhythm in a translation, even if possible, may not prove desirable. To return to the Negro spiritual discussed earlier, much of its effect lay in the conflict between heavy, sustained vowels in the first three lines and the sudden break into a spirited paeonic rhythm: "O, Mary, don't ya weep and don't ya moan." The translation turned this into slow, stress-loaded anapests "O Maria, nu plinge, nu cîrîi." Since we associate anapests with light, comic poems, we may be surprised that they should yield such a mournful sound. I've no idea what Romanians expect from such triple meters; Russian poets use them for their heaviest and most serious poems. (So could we, I suspect, if we learned to stress-load them as did the Romanian lecturer.) But whatever meter a translator finds, readers' expectations will have to be reckoned with, as well as new constructs of sounds, tones and linguistic complexities.

What "evaporates in translation" is the nonsense. Sadly, we seldom have enough sense, enough exciting material in our conscious thoughts to give a reader's brain much workout, much exhilaration. We need the imponderables of music, moonshine, malarkey—material withheld from the conscious language centers either because offensive to some censor or too rich and various for any narrow area of cortex. How we combine areas of conscious, near-conscious, and unconscious cognition —the semantics and syntax of the left brain with the areas of emotion and ritual of the right—is, after all, the benchmark of a psyche, a brain, a human personality.

We find in our poetry (art still imitating life) a constant tug of war between sense and nonsense. We're continually pushing more of a poem into nonsense, into those darker areas where we're still children given to the joys of communal song and dance. But, also being modern, civilized adults, we keep edging those arcane elements back toward sense.

In poems or songs, foreign languages are specially subject to misunderstanding and alteration; where such materials have been orally transmitted without the petrifying medium of print, we can closely observe this process. As the ballads, for instance, passed from one singer, one community's language, to another, what once made clear sense often passed into nonsense, yet could then re-emerge with new meanings. Such accidents are by no means always deleterious: they often permit the unconscious to come into play. Just as Freud showed that dreams, puns, word echoes, slips of the tongue, spoonerisms, false hearings, etc., may reveal our hidden thoughts, so may "faulty" translations.

In the ballad of "King Orfeo," for instance, the refrain lines may appear to be nonsense:

> Der lived a king inta da aste,
> *Scowan ürla grün*
> Der lived a lady in da wast.
> *Whar giorten han grün oarlac*

Francis James Child, however, took the first refrain to be a corruption of Danish:

> Skoven årle grön
> (Early green's the wood).

The second refrain is more puzzling; the Danish scholar Grundtvig conjectures:

> Hvor hjorten hån går årlig
> (Where the hart goes yearly).

For the Shetland Scots who sang this version and may have known Danish, these lines must have had some meaning. For us, even if we recognize the language, they remain nonsense. Still, they work almost as well that way: the refrains seldom draw directly on, or add to, the main story line, but instead provide a contrast and relief.

A similar case turns up among the troubadours. Most manuscripts give certain lines of "Farai un vers, pos mi sonelh," by Guillaume IX of Acquitaine, as nonsense,

> Ar auzire qu'ai respondut;
> Anc no li diz ni bat ni but,
> Ni fer ni fust no ai mentaugut,
>   Mas sol aitan:
> "Babariol, babariol,
>   Babarian."

Guillaume, disguised for travel, has met two married ladies who seem flirtatious, yet:

> For my reply—I'll swear to you
> I didn't tell them Bah or Boo,
> I answered nothing false or true;
>   I just said, then,
> "Babario, babariew,
>   Babarian."

Thinking he's a mute who can't tell tales, the ladies take him home for an eight-day orgy. Well and good; then we learn that one manuscript (MS C), gives a variant stanza ending

> Tarrababart
> Marta babelio riben
> Sara ma hart.

which A. R. Nykl identifies as a "reminiscence of the Syrian Arabic mixed with Turkish." He interprets the passage: "See behind the door; two women, I know; it's cold today." These lines, too, may be almost as effective if treated as the nonsense which other scholars (like the lustful ladies) take them for. Yet we may be missing some innuendo here; the Arabic *might* have made sense to Guillaume and his court—his father had once received 5,000 Arabic women, musicians and dancers in reparation for a war debt.

Translating Troubadour songs remains a problem, even when reading Shakespeare. In *As You Like It*, Amiens sings:

> Under the greenwood tree
> Who loves to lie with me,
> And turn his merry note
> Unto the sweet bird's throat,
> Come hither, come hither, come hither:
> Here shall he see
> No enemy
> But winter and rough weather.

The melancholy Jacques responds with his own parodic verse:

> If it do come to pass
> That any man turn ass,
> Leaving his wealth and ease
> A stubborn will to please,
> Ducdame, ducdame, ducdame:
> Here shall he see
> Gross fools as he,
> And if he will come to me.

Asked, "What's that 'ducdame'," Jacques replies, "'Tis a Greek invocation, to call fools into a circle." Learned publications, over the years, have printed ever more ingenious conjectures—e.g., that it is a misspelling of "duc ad me" meaning "lead him to me." Familiarity with early song reveals that the misogynist Jacques is mocking the troubadour (or troubadour-influenced) lover who might sing "Douce Dame" hoping to please the stubborn will of his sweet lady and so insert himself into her most private "circle" (Machaut's "Douce Dame Jolie" being the best known such song). Here, certainly, decay toward nonsense has damaged an important text.

By definition, macaronic verse and song includes bits and echoes of other languages.

Amo, amas, I love a lass
Like a cedar tall and slender;
Sweet cowslip's Grace
Is her nominative case
And she's of the feminine gender.
　Rorum, corum, angelorum,
　Harem, scarem, divo. . . .

A more extreme example runs:

Civili derego fortibus inero.
Demes nobus demes trux.
('See, Willy, dere dey go, forty buses in a row.'
'Dem is no buses, dem is trucks.')

Latin is favored for mock slogans such as General "Vinegar Joe"
Stillwell's

Illegitimi non Carborundum
(Don't let the bastards grind you down.)

or the roguish motto attributed to various American political figures:

Orchide forum trahite, cordes et mentes veniant.
(Grab 'em by the balls; the hearts and minds will follow.)

Latin, of course, often serves more serious purposes. Sir Thomas
Wyatt, in a well-known poem (itself an imitation of Petrarch), tells
of his vain pursuit of a lady, perhaps Anne Boleyn. Its climax,
coming after a series of broken, half-suspended clauses, hurls a
Latin phrase at us:

Whoso list to hunt I know where is an hind;
　But as for me, helas, I may no more:
　The vain travail hath wearied me so sore,
　I ame of them that farthest cometh behind.
Yet may I by no means my wearied mynde

103

> Drawe from the Deer: but as she fleeth afore
> Fainting I follow; I leave off therefore,
> Sithens in a net I seek to hold the wind.
> Who list her hunt I put him out of doubt,
>   As well as I may spend his time in vain:
>   And graven with diamonds in letters plain
> There is written her fair neck round about:
> *'Noli me tangere* for Cesars I ame,
>   And wild for to hold though I seem tame.'

Wyatt's contemporaries, knowing both Latin and the Bible, would swiftly have recognized the risen Jesus' words: "Do not touch me for I am not yet risen unto my father." For us, it is almost as if the poet had been so moved as to speak "in tongues." Yet serious modern readers, too, will recognize that the creature Wyatt portrays, commanding the powers of both Christ and Caesar (i.e., Henry VIII), is both too holy to touch and too profane. For such readers, this poem may actually have improved in progressing toward nonsense—taking longer to identify that daring quotation may help one realize the creature's fierce intangibility.

One would expect texts of reasonably sense-laden prose to be translatable: we welcome our Latin *Winni Ille Pu* or the Russian *Vinni-Pukh i vse-vse-vse*. Poems which involve dialects or nonsense might seem untranslatable. On one visit to the Romanian Writers' Union, I was amazed to find some members translating Berryman's *Dream Songs*—still unknown at that time to most American readers. What equivalent could there be for all that baby talk, the tough guy lingo, the stage Negro dialect? These days, international scholars translating *Finnegans Wake* must first decide what languages they're translating *from*.

Nonetheless, some of our finest translations have been from nonsense and near-nonsense verse. Lewis Carroll's "The Hunting of the Snark" has been rendered into Latin elegiacs as well as Virgilian hexameters; into Italian, Swedish, Danish, Spanish, twice into German, twice into Dutch and thrice into French. And Carroll's "Jabberwocky," depending so heavily on portmanteau nonsense, is just the sort of challenge poets and translators cannot resist. It has provoked a version in French, two in Latin (one by Carroll's uncle), and, probably the best of all, in German.

DER JAMMERWOCK

Es brillig war. Die schlichten Toven
  Wirrten and wimmelten in Waben;
Und Aller-Mümsige Burggoven
  Die mohmen Räth ausgraben.

Bewahre doch vor Jammerwoch!
  Die Zähne knirschen, Krallen kratzen!
Bewahr' vor Jubjub-Vogal, vor
  Frumiösen Banderschnätzchen! . . .

Its perpetrator, the eminent Greek scholar, Robert Scott, doubled the prank by claiming that his version was the true original and that Carroll had simply translated it into English.

Ormonde de Kay, Jr., in his 1971 *Rimes de la Mère Oie*, translated many English nursery rhymes:

Au marché, au marché,
  Achetons un porc gras.
De retour, de retour
  Au petit pas.

Au marché, au marché,
  Achetons un pourceau.
De retour, de retour
  Au petit trot.

In 1980, the same translator issued *N'Heures Souris Rames*, rendering many of the same verses into "Fractured French," recreating the sounds rather than the sense:

Tu marques et tu marques et
 Tu bâilles, effet typique.
Heaume et gaine! Heaume et gaine!
 Gigoté chic!

Tu marques et tu marques et
 Tu bâilles, effet tac.
Heaume et gaine! Heaume et gaine!
 Gigoté Jacques.

In the earlier volume ("hickory" being the same in both languages),
he had offered

Hickory, dickory, dac
Souris entend tic-tac.
 Horloge sonne l'heure,
 Souris prend peur
Hickory, dickory, dac.

In *Mots D'Heures: Gousses Rames*, Luis d'Antin van Rooten had
already reproduced the original's sound to tell of someone who
dared laugh at the monks of Provence:

Et qui rit des curés d'Oc?
De Meuse raines, houp! de cloques.
De quelles loques ce turque coin
Et ne d'âne ni rennes,
Et qui rit des curés d'Oc.

De Kay rendered what had probably been a parable on a political
favorite's downfall:

Hompté-Dompté assis sur un mur,
Hompté-Dompté en tomba trés dur.
Ni les chevaux ni les soldats du roi
N'ont pu recoller ce grand maladroit.

Van Rooten had offered us the story of an idiot child, thus disguising, in turn, the tale of some famous political prisoner:

> Un petit d'un petit
> S'étonne aux Halles
> Un petit d'un petit
> Ah! degrés te fallent
> Indolent qui ne sort cesse
> Indolent qui ne se mène
> Qu'importe un petit d'un petit
> Tout Gai de Reguennes.

Or, if that does not seem sufficiently far-fetched, we may turn to the German version from John Hulme's *Moerder Guss Reims:*

> Um die Dumm' die Saturn Aval;
> Um die Dumm' die Ader Grät fahl
> Alter ging's Ohr säss und Alter ging's mähen.
> Kuh denn "putt" um Dieter Gitter er gähn'.

which he glosses as the story of "a foolish Greek maiden [who] becomes embroiled with the supernatural and is rescued . . . by being turned into a cow."

Still in German, the contemporary poet Ernst Jandl does much the same in a "surface translation" of Wordsworth's "My heart leaps up when I behold a rainbow in the sky."

oberflaechenuebersetzung

> mai hart lieb zapfen eibe hold
> er renn bohr in sees kai
> so was sieht wenn mai laeuft begehen
> so es sieht nahe emma maehen
> so biet wenn aerschel grollt
> ohr leck mit ei!
> seht steil dies fader rosse maehen

in teig kurt wisch mai desto bier
baum deutsche deutsch bajonett schur alp eiertier.

In the pursuit of nonsense, we may withdraw not only from a poem's sense, but even from its sound. Morgenstern offers us:

FISCHES NACHTGESANG

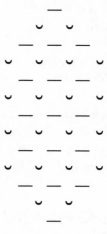

We're left with a metrical paradigm—silent, as befits a fish. Further, the scansion marks resemble closed eyelids, fish scales, or ripples on water, so adding visual rhythms to the aural, but silent, rhythm of the prosodic diagram. Max Knight gives an inspired translation:

FISH'S NIGHT SONG

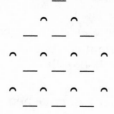

As a final step in this flight from sense, I will note that the late James Merrill used to perform this poem by opening, alternately, his lips or eyes. Whether he might have performed Max Knight's "translation" in a headstand, I dare not conjecture.

Diverting as they are, such translations of nonsense—like most translations of the dictionary meaning—are unfit to stand alone. They at least recognize that they can provide sufficient challenge and stimulation only *en face.* A poem needs, within itself, that much richness of association, of cortical fireworks. Just so, to survive on its own feet, a translation will have not only to render the poem's literal sense but also to reinvent, as best it can, its nonsense.

Octavio Paz closes his essay "Reading and Contemplation" with a Tibetan parable too pertinent not to paraphrase. For many days, the fifth Dalai Lama saw the goddess Tara circling the wall of his temple. At the same time every day, a poor old man was seen walking around the wall reciting a verse prayer to Tara. This prayer was a translation of a Sanskrit text praising perfect wisdom, which Mahayana Buddhism personalizes as this Tara, a goddess of inexpressible beauty. Theologians found, however, that the poor man was repeating a corrupted translation and taught him the correct one. From that day forth, Tara was never seen again.

III. Dialects, Babblings, Styles

Some years ago, as part of an interview, I asked the former armaments minister of the Third Reich, Albert Speer, how Hitler could have ordered into Germany's final battles units which everyone else knew had been disabled or destroyed. In answer, Speer recalled that a friend of his, a cancer specialist who'd predicted that he himself would die of that disease, did not recognize, when they appeared, his own obvious symptoms. Speer summed up: "He neglected his knowing"—a phrase so revealing that I "liberated" it for use in a poem. Had he been more fluent in English, Speer might have said, "He repressed that knowledge" or "He fooled himself"—phrases worn past immediacy or extension, thus offering some lowest common denominator of meaning and sending the hearer on his way. Difficulty with the language may have led Speer to say more than he'd intended: suggesting not only his Führer's dereliction but also his own.

Speer was, in effect, creating his own dialect in a less than native language. One's own tongue, since it implies belonging, may well foster security and numbed perceptions. Familiarity breeds, if not contempt, at least inattention; what alerts us more sharply than fear? Distrust of other dialects must once have been essential to survival; remnants of tribal or parental xenophobias still make us a little nervous when we "torque wet strainers." It *is* a strain, puts a torque on our wits—demands that we pursue meanings down unfamiliar paths.

Yet that may have advantages. Isn't it a good deal more fun to read the old Robin Hood ballads without an editor's modernizations?

> In somer, when the shawes be sheyne,
>   And leves be large and long,
> Hit is full mery in feyre foreste
>   To here the foulys song.

Not only do we demonstrate mental dexterity by cracking a code; we call up some flavor of a time when spelling was less regularized, more sensible and meaningful. Besides, anything we've invested with time and effort becomes more securely our own: the added miniseconds allow images to concretize and more surely realize themselves.

Dialects, with their awkward precisions, may have a place in poetry, after all; there *are* reputable examples. Shakespeare presents Doctor Caius and Sir Hugh Evans of *Merry Wives of Windsor*, or the Captains Fluellen, Macmorris, and Jamy of *Henry V*. Every Christmas season our church or college choirs sweetly sing Orlando di Lasso's "Matona mia cara." Few of the singers recognize this as a *tedesco*—one of many Italian songs mocking the German mercenaries left to scrounge about the countryside after one war or another. Here, one such soldier strums a guitar (*don-don-don, diri-diri, don-don, don-don*), trying to serenade a lady. His fractured Italian (e.g., "Matona" for "Madonna") and his notable loutishness turn his song comically indelicate:

> I'll be your sturdy fellow
> If you don't take me wrong;
> Stout like a ram I'll bellow
> And hump you all night long.
>> *Dong-dong-dong*
>> *Dearie, Dearie, Dong-dong,*
>> *Dong-dong.*

Dialects, however, may well imitate without mockery, may identify sympathetically with some subculture, or with an individual voice from a subculture. We have the folkish poems of Thomas Hardy or William Barnes, the Scots verses of Hugh MacDiarmid, translations by Tom Scott or W. S. Milne. Among our Black poets, obvious examples come from Gwendolyn Brooks and the underrated Robert Hayden.

In "Reading and Contemplation," Octavio Paz recounts the story of the Tower of Babel and how God punished a prideful humanity by splitting it into diverse language groups:

> The beginning of plurality was also the beginning of
> history: empires, wars, and the great piles of rubble

that civilizations have left. Babel is the Hebrew version of Babylon, and the condemnation of that city, probably the first cosmopolitan city in history, is the condemnation of cosmopolitanism, of plural and pluralist society that acknowledges the existence of the other and of others.

Poetry must once have been a tribal expression, a ceremony of group solidarity: "We're better than those clods over there." The accepted language, familiar technical devices, the verbal music, the babble and mumbo jumbo all carried a clear, single meaning: acceptance of and by the group. As our society has grown, forcing conformity upon larger and larger masses, we have developed more methods of coercion: force, censorship, news control, mass media, school programs, forms of parenting. Difference in language has come to be seen not as something we've been punished *with*, but as something we can be punished *for*. Meantime, the arts, poetry in particular, have developed into a tool for the investigation of, and empathy with, otherness. They have come to speak for the subculture and the individual against the greater society's drives and values, the standard language with its suppressions and neglects.

Dialect poems or songs, evading our usual censorships, offer a triumph over the internalized parent-censors. As with other poetic devices, we reach a meaning through connotations, sound effects, rhythms—the associations of the right brain—admitting responses normally inhibited by the left brain's denotations. The mathematician Stanislaw Ulam said that the purpose of rhyme is to prod the mind outside its usual channels—true enough, unless the rhymes have become so worn and secondhand that they now are *part* of the usual channels. The same is true (with the same proviso) of other poetic devices—meter, stanzaic form, language levels and textures, archaic diction, tortured usage—stimulants that lure the mind beyond normal message content, beyond good advice, political enticement or excuse, smug membership. Even puns help jar us from our torpor. The journeying soul, once a mysterious, holy entity, has been transformed into the bottom of your foot. Unlike the

112

proper Ms. Hood we cross the forest on paths forbidden, fall into bad company; yield ourselves to a life sparked by some "wicket woofs" and "strainers"—the dangers and excitements our neural systems were designed for.

As the conventional techniques came to be more and more associated with sentimental verse, advertising jingles, or popular songs—the expectable sounds and sentiments of the commercial tribe—the search for new techniques has engaged many writers with such games and riddles as we've been considering, with anagrams, typography, palindromes: "Madam, I'm Adam," or "Rats live on no evil star." It is easier, though, to discard old techniques than it is to invent new ones. New devices—each invented by a specific brain for a specific aesthetic problem – can quickly turn into new conventions, new rules, predictable and dulling. Applied arbitrarily from outside, they subtract from the dictionary sense rather than enriching it.

Most such searches reveal little about either our worlds or our minds—but so do most efforts at conventional poetry. In the right hands, they may prove not merely clever, but may approach wisdom. Consider the kind of poem Robert Morgan calls "Spore Prose":

MOUNTAIN GRAVEYARD
—for the author of "Slow Owls"

stone notes
slate tales
sacred cedars

heart earth
asleep please
hated death

Here, anagrams do just what Ulam says rhyme should do. Whether another poet (including Jonathan Williams, who wrote "Slow Owls") can use such a device for further creative ends waits to be discovered in the individual psyche. We do see a related device in a poem of Robert Francis's which traces out a rural life not with anagrams but with a list of "solid compounds":

SILENT POEM

backroad leafmold stonewall chipmunk
underbrush grapevine woodchuck shadblow

woodsmoke cowbarn honeysuckle woodpile
sawhorse bucksaw outhouse wellsweep

backdoor flagstone bulkhead buttermilk
candlestick ragrug firedog brownbread

hilltop outcrop cowbell buttercup
whetstone thunderstorm pitchfork steeplebush

gristmill millstone cornmeal waterwheel
watercress buckwheat firefly jewelweed

gravestone groundpine windbreak bedrock
weathercock snowfall starlight cockcrow

The technique, which forgoes normal English syntax, reminds me of Anglo-Saxon runes or of a Cubist painting. Each compound noun carries two stresses, so recording not only visual objects but also their passage through time—though they remain, themselves, immoveable and individual as cinder blocks.

We have long used visual images in creating poems. Early examples come from George Herbert's "Easter Wings" and "The Altar;" recent ones from Dylan Thomas and John Hollander. *Vers concret* has tried to make the poem's concrete shape its chief vehicle and matter. This often produces something at best clever, at worst cute. A remarkable exception, however, is by Cummings:

l(a

le
af
fa

ll

s)

one
l

iness

The eccentric typography not only depicts the leaf dipping and
sliding through the air then flattening onto the ground, but it also
underlines a sense of isolation: the similarity of the letter *l* to the
numeral 1, the isolation of the word "one" in line 7, the "I-ness" or
sealed individuation of the last line. Cummings also provides a way
to read the poem aloud as a rebus: we must supply positional words
to create syntax. Interpreting his parentheses, we read, "A leaf falls
in loneliness" or "In loneliness a leaf falls." The crux is that it *may* be
read, sound being the essential material of poems—using a part of
the mind developed well before the visual.

Nonsense phrases and riddles, too, offer new trails, unsanctioned
destinations. Robert Austerlitz, a scholar of Eastern European linguis-
tics, once remarked that nonsense syllables in songs, *fa-la-la-la, down-a-
down-a-down, hi-diddle-dum,* always have one meaning: *Expletive De-
leted.* Syllables that stir forbidden sexual meanings are readily found:

A lusty young smith at his vice stood a-filing,
His hammer laid by but his forge still aglow,
When to him a buxom young damsel came smiling
And asked if to work at her forge he would go.
  With a jingle-bang, jingle-bang, jingle-bang, jingle,
  With a jingle-bang, jingle-bang, jingle, hi-ho!

We less willingly attend to our knowledge that love (as opposed to lust) may be neither what we asked for nor what was promised; that requires some wilier nonsense, as in this English song:

THE TAILOR AND THE MOUSE

There was a tailor loved a mouse;
    Hi diddle dum, come feed, ah.
They lived together in one house.
    Hi diddle dum, come feed.
    Hi diddle dum, come tarum, tantrum
        Through the town of Ramsay,
    Hi diddle dum, come over the lea;
    Hi diddle dum, come feed, ah.

The tailor had a tall silk hat;
The mouse he swallowed it—fancy that!

The tailor thought that his mouse was ill;
He gave him half of a nasty pill.

The tailor thought that his mouse would die;
He baked him in an apple pie.

The pie was cut and the mouse ran out;
The tailor followed him all about.

The tailor found that his mouse was dead
    Hi diddle dum, come feed, ah,
So he bought him another one in its stead.
    Hi diddle dum, come feed.
    Hi diddle dum, come tarum, tantrum
        Through the town of Ramsay,
    Hi diddle dum, come over the lea;
    Hi diddle dum, come feed, ah.

Though we usually reprint refrains only at the beginning and end of stanzaic songs, if those "nonsense" lines are not read (or better, sung) throughout, a song's implications leach away. Without the connotations of *"diddle," "come over the lea"* and *"tarum, tantrum,"* without reminders of *"mouse"* as an endearment, *"come feed"* would remain merely a summons to a pet animal. We lose the inkling that lovers, driven by ancient hungers, may devour not only each other's dignity—their tall silk hats—but each other. In tantrums of revenge, they may embed each other in terminal domestic comforts. Yet if their "mouse" tried to escape, they'd pursue him or her all over town; if relentless nurture proved fatal, they would soon buy a new victim to adore.

Bitter insights for such a lively little song. But none of this is asserted or enforced; the singer can call us gloom-bound academics or Freudians who've foisted horrid suggestions upon his innocent ditty—like the man who, on being told that his Rorschach test indicates he is sex-obsessed, objects, "But you're the one that showed me those dirty pictures!" And, of course, songs or poems may convey meanings beyond the conscious grasp of either singer or hearer. They aim not only to display "dirty" words and sexual forbiddances but to uncover deeper, more extensive repressions, to think the unthinkable.

In England, "Don-don-don, diri, diri, don" might become "Down, down, down, derry derry, down"—pleasant gibberish that often lightens and balances a sad or violent song. To paraphrase G. K. Chesterton, a typical ballad might run: "The miller he went home to his wife / And cut off her head with his wee pen knife. / With a fa, la, derry derry, down." The melody of the traditional "Three Ravens," however, gives this refrain a mournful cast which seems, at first, to emphasize the tragic sense of the story:

THREE RAVENS

There were three ravens sat on a tree,
  Down-a-down, hey down, hey down;
They were as black as they might be,

117

> *With a down;*
> The one of them said to his mate,
> *Down*
> Where shall we our breakfast take?
> *With a down, derry, derry, derry, down, down.*

> Down, down in yonder greene field
> There lies a knight slain under his shield;
> His hawks they flie so eagerly,
> There's no fowl dare come him nigh.

> His hounds they lie down at his feet,
> So well can they their master keep;
> Down there comes a fallow doe
> Great with young as she might go.

> She lifted up his bloody head
> And kist his wounds that were so red;
> She got him up upon her back,
> And carried him to earthen lake.

> She buried him before the prime,
> *Down-a-down, hey down, hey down;*
> She was dead herself ere evensong time,
> *With a down;*
> Then God send every gentleman
> *Down*
> Such hawkes, such hounds, and such a leman
> *With a down, derry, derry, derry, down, down.*

The refrains—again, all must be sung or spoken—constantly slide into active meaning. At first, "down" might suggest only a desire to bring the carrion birds from their height or, conversely, suggest the ravens' attraction to the corpse. Soon, though, it implies the actions of the hawks and hounds guarding the body—perhaps even the hounds' recollection of their master's command. Later, it helps depict the doe's struggle to lift, then bury the knight's body;

finally, it invests the prayer that God send "down" such loyal followers (human or animal) to us all.

This "nonsense" turns the ballad, despite its tragic action and mournful melody, toward hope. It's always been clear that we will die, that we might be betrayed, "slain under [our] shield." The refrain's implications expand and underline the chance that, despite this world's beastly appetites and treacheries, some of our values may survive in those we've loved—that, with luck, we may depend on those who've depended on us.

Such refrains, however, may convey meanings less hopeful. Some years ago I translated the Romanian ballad "Mesterul Manole"—the story of the master builder Manole or Emmanuel. On pain of death, he and twelve fellow masons have been commanded by the prince, Negru Voda, to erect a great monastery as his memorial. Yet all they build by day falls that same night. A dream reveals that they must sacrifice whichever wife or sister first comes bringing their food. To Manole's horror, his beloved wife arrives first; he must build her into the edifice. Ensuring that the masons will not construct an equally proud memorial for someone else, Negru Voda orders the masons left to die on the rooftop. Manole, remembering his wife's voice calling him, falls unconscious from the roof to his death.

This ballad, known by type as "The Walled-Up Wife," is found throughout the countries and languages of central Europe. The story is not merely a fiction: through all this area, excavations have uncovered human bones in the foundations of ancient buildings. Most often these are the bones of children; at later sites, bones of dogs or other animals substituted for human sacrifices, as in the biblical story of Abraham and Isaac. I have seen Greek masons kill a chicken to embed in a house foundation; fairly recent newspaper stories told of a man killed and buried in a dam in India and of another in Africa executed for building someone into a church.

Working on my translation, I wondered why there was no version in English. Then I recalled something ballad scholars noticed long ago:

London Bridge is falling down
Falling down, falling down;
London Bridge is falling down
My fair lady.

Build it up with iron bars,
Iron bars . . .

Iron bars will break and bend,
Break and bend . . .

Build it up with silver and gold,
Silver and gold . . .

Silver and gold will not hold,
Will not hold . . .

Here's a prisoner we have brought,
My fair lady.

Take the key and lock her up,
Lock her up, lock her up;
Take the key and lock her up,
My fair lady.

Children act out this song's little drama, even build their arms into a cage for one playmate, yet do not ask how the refrain, "My fair lady," relates to problems of bridge collapse. At first, the phrase might specify who the song addresses, or may serve as nonsense, like "Fa-la-la" or "derry, derry, down." Later, though the phrase openly tells the children that their captive is the one ingredient which can shore up the bridge, they still sing it as empty babble. Yet they must feel they are acting out some momentous act—implying that nothing significant can be built without the sacrifice of other things held dear. Why else would the song have survived so long?

Thus, our willingness to admit nonsense sometimes allows meanings which, undiguised, would be intercepted and rejected, to slip past the conscious mind. Conversely, we may become so used to thinking poems mean other than what they say that we ignore the things they do say. Thus, the greatest of the Scottish ballads:

EDWARD

"Why dois your brand sae drap wi' bluid,
　　Edward, Edward?
Why dois your brand sae drap wi' bluid,
　　And why sae sad gang ye, O?"
"O I hae kill'd my hauke sae guid,
　　Mither, mither,
O I hae killed my hauke sae guid,
　　And I had nae mair bot hee, O."

"Your haukis bluid was nevir sae reid,
　　My deir son, I tell thee, O."
"O I hae killed my reid-roan steid,
　　That erst was sae fair and sae frie, O."

Your steid was auld, and ye hae gat mair,
　　Sum other dule ye drie, O."
"I hae kill'd my ain fadir deir,
　　Alas, and wae is mee, O!"

"And whatten penance wul ye drie for that,
　　My deir son, now tell me, O."
"Ile set my feit in yonder boat,
　　And I'll gang ovir the sea, O."

"And what wul ye doe wi' your towirs and your ha',
　　That were sae fair to see, O?"
"Ile let thame stand tul they doun fa',
　　For here nevir mair maun I bee, O."

> "And what wul ye leive to your bairns and your wife,
> When ye gang ovir the sea, O?"
> "The warldis room, late them beg thrae life,
> For thame nevir mair wul I see, O."
>
> "And what wul ye leive to your ain mither deir,
> *Edward, Edward?*
> What wul ye leive to your ain mither deir,
> My deir son, now tell me, O?"
> "The curse of hell frae me sall ye beir,
> *Mither, mither,*
> The curse of hell frae me sall ye beir,
> Sic counseils ye gave to me, O!"

On first reading, most of us reach the last stanza with no sense of what's been going on. We have accepted what amounts to nonsense—have let ourselves be persuaded that a Scottish lord might keep only one hawk, that his mother can distinguish hawk's blood from any other kind, that she might accept so impassively the news that her son has just killed his father. Now we must reconsider every sentence. Yet however much we realize the mother and son's struggle for control over towers and hall, we never completely obliterate the action we saw first. Choosing between layers of meaning implies admitting both—providing a richer workout for our responses, a chance to fire off simultaneous patterns of synapses, a fuller recognition of our world's complexity.

Meaning to denigrate Milton's style, Dr. Johnson called it "a Babylonish dialect." Speaking for the neoclassical period, which had devised its own "poetic language," Johnson faults Milton for using a language virtually his own. But isn't that, actually, its virtue? Wasn't Dante, too, writing in an outlandish tongue? Only the great authority such writers have later acquired, and the number of their imitators, make them now seem central and "standard." At a concert, we suffer from that same dulling of difference, of vitality, when we listen to Beethoven, even to Debussy, unless we can relearn how outlandish their harmonies sounded when new.

A personal style is, in effect, a "dialect," one symbol of a unique human character. Demanding extra effort, more adventurousness from a reader or listener, it promises to take us to meanings via new pathways, to restore more of that knowing we've neglected. In the modern arts, we confirm membership in an elite that not only likes puzzles but savors a tougher riddle: the variety of human being. We seek the poem not to lose identity by melding with any group but rather to extend our own identity by savoring the differences of others, most immediately that one other symbolized by the style of the poem in hand—in short, we're seeking a new "Babylonish" dialect. We want the individual oddities, the towering babble and Babel that free us from our Babylon's uniformity. We want the skewed syntax of Cummings:

> anyone lived in a pretty how town
> (with up so floating many bells down)
> spring summer autumn winter
> he sang his didn't he danced his did

the stately music of Pound:

> What thou lovest well remains
> What thou lovest well is thy true heritage,
> What thou lovest well shall not be reft from thee.

or William Carlos Williams's line breaks, which deliberately conflict with the syntactic unit and force us to fight for the meaning:

> By the road to the contagious hospital
> under the surge of the blue
> mottled clouds driven from the
> northeast—a cold wind. Beyond, the
> waste of broad, muddy fields
> brown with dried weeds, standing and fallen

Even more, we ask not so much for dialect, the language of a subgroup, as for a style, the language and manner that symbolizes a personality. Surely this is what we seek and find in the poems of Emily Dickinson:

> A narrow Fellow in the Grass
> Occasionally rides —
> You may have met Him — did you not
> His notice sudden is —

We could easily "translate" this into our standard language:

> Sometimes, a slender creature
> Glides through the grass;
> Perhaps you have seen him, but if not,
> He moves quite rapidly.

What has "evaporated" is the tart personality, the eccentricity of syntax, usage, and construction, the surprising slant rhyme, that slight disjunction from standard practice. Others have commented on the "*s*" sounds, the hint of a hiss in the fourth line. The inverted syntax is even more important; "His notice is sudden" would lose the force of "is"—a word usually unstressed which is now thrown into the stanza's most frequently and fully stressed position where it also fails to fulfill our expectation of a rhyme. Ironically, the snake's existence (his sudden *is*-ness) is emphasized by that unorthodox syntax and stress, its refusal to behave expectably. Further, we have some doubt about what "is": "His notice" could mean either our taking note of him, his giving us notice of his presence (by moving, hissing, or rising), or even giving us notice (like a renter) of his departure. In that tiny phrase, lies a little scene where three things happen almost simultaneously.

We value Dickinson for that style, those warpings of normal usage, those benchmarks of individuality. Just as our style in manner, dress, and behavior is defined by what we accept or discard of our society's conventions, Dickinson's eccentricities offer the fact of otherness, an unpredictable personality, a wider humanity. This requires, however, an acceptance of the fearful magnitude of our differences. The standard language, like the prescriptive critic or the political censor, can narrow and disguise that breadth and possibly dangerous variety.

Several years ago, *The New Yorker* published an excerpt from a Japanese novel, *What the Maid Saw,* by Yasutaka Tsutsui:

> Katsumi had come across the image of the peach in
> a poem by an American Poet.
>
>> The years are taking their toll.
>> It's time to roll up the cuffs of my pants—
>> Time to part my hair from the back—
>> Time to eat peaches.
>> I put on my white flannel pants and walked on the
>>   beach.
>> I heard mermaids singing to each other.
>> Mermaids who would never sing out to me.

Despite one or two actual errors, we have here, essentially, the dictionary sense of T. S. Eliot's "Prufrock"—though divorced from his voice by its redoubled translation back into English. That voice resided in the nonsense of the poem—all those technical and stylistic effects which, since we stopped singing our poems, take music's place in extending the language beyond the range of daily discourse. These effects give the original an amazing emotional range, a complete and accurate portrait of a wily mind protecting itself from the dangers of courtship:

> I grow old ... I grow old ...
> I shall wear the bottoms of my trousers rolled.

The first line, seemingly a lament, is really an excuse. Eliot himself suggested that Prufrock might be no older than twenty-three (his age, incidentally, when he finished the poem). The next line is even more startling in rhyme and rhythm than in its details. Seemingly free verse, it is actually based on the four-foot, heavy-stress lines of such nursery rhymes as "Hot Cross Buns" or "Three Blind Mice." Even more apt, echoing Prufrock's rhyme on "old," is

> Pease porridge hot; pease porridge cold;
> Pease porridge in the pot, nine days old.

We've already heard surprising musics from Prufrock; his habitual excuses and delays had earlier developed into a rhythm like an operetta's patter song:

> Do I dare
> Disturb the universe?
> In a minute there is time
> For decisions and revisions which a minute will reverse.

In the passage "translated" above, Prufrock shrank his universe to a peach:

> Shall I part my hair behind? Do I dare to eat a peach?
> I shall wear white flannel trousers, and walk upon the
>   beach.

Here stress-loading, rhymes and echoes— "hair / dare / wear" and "eat / peach / beach"—weight and slow the bouncy movement. Yet if we broke those lines according to their syntax

> Shall I part my hair behind?
> Do I dare to eat a peach?
> I shall wear white flannel trousers,
> And walk upon the beach.

we would again hear an underlying folk rhythm:

> Cock a doodle doo,
> My dame has lost her shoe;
> My master's lost his fiddling stick
> And doesn't know what to do.
>
> If you haven't got a penny,
> A ha'-penny'll do;
> If you haven't got a ha-penny
> God bless you.

Just as Prufrock had earlier imaged his morning coat as a kind of protective shell against the ladies' scorn, he now projects an idyllic image of himself, armored by the luxury of white flannels, strolling contentedly in sexless old age on the beach. The association of the sea as the ancient symbol of feminine energy and sexuality, however, breaks the idyllic tone and music with an unexpected third rhyme and a wail of genuine despair:

I have heard the mermaids singing, each to each.

followed by a collapse into nearly comic self-pity:

I do not think that they will sing to me.

These two lines abandon the songlike folk rhythm for a strict iambic pentameter, the meter we associate with weightier emotions. No such climax (or, more fittingly, anticlimax), none of those reflections of personal character, are heard in the translated "sense." That records *what* Prufrock says; his psyche must be interpreted from the *how* and the *why* of his saying.

Patients with damage to areas of the right brain (which correspond to the language areas of the left) can still understand the message content of statements; they cannot understand or express emotional content. We can justly call such a translation half-witted, half-brained.

Oedipus boasted of his ability to solve riddles. He'd done pretty well with the Sphinx's: "What goes on four legs in the morning, two legs in the daytime, and three legs in the evening?" That's an abstract, impersonal riddle—"What is Man?"—requiring only cleverness, the recognition that "morning" means early in one's life, not early in the day. When the oracle at Delphi told him he would lie with his mother and kill his father, he faced a deeper, personal riddle demanding insight, wisdom; cleverness only helped evade the solution. The answer was not to flee his home but, rather, not to sleep with older, prominent women, not to kill older, arrogant men—even, possibly, not to kill *anyone*. He neglected the implied question about his personal tendencies in sex and violence: "Who are you?"

127

The riddles we've considered—rebuses, eccentric spellings, invented dialects, anguish languish, knock-knocks, resonances, etc.—are, as suggested, verbal jungle gyms where we can develop an agility for connotations, suggestions, implications. They ask us to consider the very real problem of differences and similarities in the world: "What's the difference between a snake and a goose?" The answer then shifts the problem to another area of concern, ambiguities and transpositions of language: "A snake is an asp in the grass." Such riddle imply that the question has a single correct answer and, moreover, may be shrugged off if we can just locate the right mode and a clever (preferably raunchy) formulation. It may well be the comforting voice of our doting "groinmurder" – or the "wicket woof's" handpuppet of her head—telling us we need not worry our little heads about the qualities of our world. The poem is concerned with fiercer enigmas, deeper censorships; Sphinx-like, it always asks who we are—questions our similarity to and difference from the mind portrayed by style and content. No clever shift of mode will satisfy that inquisition; to grasp another mind will require all channels of perception, all our versatility of association.

Perhaps we can alter Frost's dictum that poetry is about the problems that have no answer. More accurately, poems—like the subjects they address—have no *one* answer; they may have as many answers as answerers. As readers, we must form, out of a poem's materials, our own "translation," our own understanding, reflecting the idiosyncracies not only of the writer's cortical organization, but also of our own. The wider the areas of meaning a work of art accesses, the greater the range of responses it will touch off in various readers. Why else do we concern ourselves with how others (friends, critics, scholars) experience a work of art with "readings" which may oppose (and so enrich) our own? Such considerations merely confirm Picasso's assertion that art is always an act of aggression, or Morse Peckham's that "the role of the artist demands that he construct perceptual fields which offer a disorienting experience."

Having started with a children's tale, why not end with one? I began with a riddle whose answer was "Little Red Riding Hood." I end with one from Joyce's story of "The Ondt and the Gracehoper" in *Finnegans Wake*; being a poem, its riddle may well have as many answers as hearers, each answer being one mind's unique reformation of the question.

> I forgive you, grondt Ondt, said the Gracehoper, weeping,
> For the sukes of the sakes you are safe in whose keeping.
> Teach Floh and Luse polkas, show Bienie where's sweet
> And be sure Vespatilla fines fat ones to heat.
> As I once played the piper I must now pay the count
> So saida to Moyhammlet and marhaba to your Mount! . . .
> I pick up your reproof, the horsegift of a friend,
> For the prize of your save is the price of my spend. . . .
> We are Wastenot with Want, precondamned, two and true,
> Till Nolans go volants and Bruneyes come blue. . . .
> My in risible universe youdly haud find
> Sulch oxtrabeeforeness meat soveal behind.
> Your feats end enormous, your volumes immense
> (May the Graces I hoped for sing your Ondtship song sense!),
> Your genus its worldwide, your spacest sublime!
> But, Holy Saltmartin, why can't you beat time?

In the name of the former and of the latter and of their holocaust. Allmen.

WHITMAN'S SELFSONG

"Whitman was more man than you'll ever be," said my student, "and more bitch, too." Neat as that, he'd snagged an essence, the uniquely positive character of Walt Whitman's sexual and literary presence: not that he refused to be a man, but that he insistently went on also being a woman. Gay Wilson Allen called him "omnisexual"; Keatsians might term his capability not so much "negative" as "positron." Whitman seems proof against our common fear that any definition will be diminishing—a fear that itself demeans us. Defining the self by its range of identifications, he insisted that he *was* whatever he encountered. This affirmation charged not only his weltanschauung but also the structure and style of his major works. True, his beliefs failed at times to overcome a sense of isolation and despair—may at times have helped cause or intensify them. Yet, despite periods of despondency, his work conveys a sense of sweeping and triumphant acceptance.

I want to investigate here the emanation of those beliefs from Whitman's life and experience, but, more significantly, their reflection in his poetic structure and style. Though I will focus on "Song of Myself," the first and greatest issuance of those beliefs and of their consequent stylistic methods, from time to time I will also cite other works for corroboration or contrast.

I. DILEMMA AND DOCTRINE

Recent studies suggests that Whitman may have suffered a devastating public disgrace in his early twenties, while teaching school in Southold, Long Island. Inconclusive evidence exists that, accused of sodomy with a student, he was first denounced from the pulpit, then may have been tarred, feathered and ridden out of town on a rail. However credible the evidence, reports of a scandal persist. Whitman himself told of trouble with the villagers in several places where he'd taught, alluding to "one period in my life of which my friends know nothing" and to "the one big factor, entanglement (I might almost say tragedy) about which I have not yet talked." The real issue, I suggest, is not whether such an incident occurred, but rather that Whitman would have passed much of his life under the threat of exposure and public ignominy and that this possibility would be likely to have far-reaching consequences for his thought and work.

We have definite evidence of only one other sexual relation in Whitman's early life—during his 1848 sojourn as an editor in New Orleans. Once thought to have been an affair with a well-born woman of mixed race, the encounter is now recognized as homosexual. Two poems (both subject to interpretation) are our only substantiation for this affair. Whether factual or invented, this relationship (unlike that in Long Island) seems replete in admiration and satisfaction.

Both relationships seem probable; yet even if both proved imaginary, we would still see here an emotional progression which, at least until recently, would have been common to most American homosexual males. We would expect Whitman to discover, early on, that his desires threatened disgrace or violence; this possibility alone might cause a retreat into isolation or into covert relationships. Developing and maintaining contacts in some homosexual subculture, he would probably resort to disguise or stealth in approaching the broader community.

We may never know the facts about Whitman's erotic contacts—whether he had sex with students, with the young men listed in his notebooks, with his retarded brother (as Paul Zweig seems to hint), even with the woman suggested by David Reynolds. It's questionable what purpose such knowledge could serve, yet we seem unable to leave off speculations. We do know, on the other hand, the nature of Whitman's desires and fantasies. It is there, I think, that we must seek what Ralph Waldo Emerson called the "long foreground" to *Leaves of Grass*.

Critics have long puzzled over this period—between, say, 1847 and 1855 (ages 28 through 36) when *Leaves of Grass* first appeared—

during which time Whitman, a hack journalist and editor, an ineffectual politician, a writer of poor stories and poorer poems, a sometime printer, schoolteacher or carpenter-builder, transformed himself into our greatest poet. I see this "long foreground," instead, as reaching back to 1841 when, aged 22, he left Long Island. It seems typical that Whitman, whom many thought lazy and devoid of purpose, should pursue this course so long and steadily. Despite his indolent appearance, we know that he doggedly followed the same drives and urges all his life.

Is it not conceivable that the greater an early humiliation—especially to one who had expressed a determination to make his life noteworthy—the greater might be his drive toward some noteworthy achievement to rescue his image in his own eyes and the world's? Why imagine that such a momentous transformation could be worked in a shorter period or by a less massive intention? We are witness here to a masterstroke of psychic engineering which ingeniously reshaped menacing forces into a rich creative resource. Attempted by a lesser psyche, this might easily have led to schizophrenia or derangement.

After 1841, the year of his purported disgrace, Whitman gave up teaching, left Long Island for Brooklyn and then Manhattan, establishing himself there as a printer and journalist. Meantime, he occasionally published poetry and short fictions, among them a story, "The Child's Champion," probably a sentimental vision of his involvement with his Long Island student. The story also prefigures the relationships his later poems would envisage, with himself as teacher-lover and the reader as his "elève" or loving disciple. During this same period, Whitman began his re-education for some greater career. Scholars have traced the process fairly completely: his broad reading in world literature, history, mythology, science and travel, the development of his tastes in music, theater and the fine arts; his investigations into phrenology, Egyptology, religious movements and politics.

By the age of twenty-six, then, Whitman had made a substantial if ordinary life in Manhattan. Like many, he lived in boardinghouses; if he lost newspaper jobs, he readily found others, gradually reaching positions of some prestige. Further progress, however, demanded two major decisions, one about his place and manner of living, the second about the application of those talents and beliefs he was so assiduously cultivating. The choices he made—each of which might seem to prohibit any wide recognition or prominence—took shape gradually, and neither may have been fully conscious or intentional.

First, Whitman returned from Manhattan to his family in Brooklyn. On and off since the age of fourteen, he had lived apart while working as a printer's apprentice or a teacher. This decision cannot have been easy: the family was wracked by poverty, dissension, illness and neurosis. Whitman had quarreled with his father, now beginning to fail; his mother, whom he so often described as "perfect," was actually querulous, demanding and constantly discontented. Of seven siblings, two succumbed to madness, one died young, while a fourth was retarded and perhaps epileptic. Assuming such responsibilities would seem to rule out anything beyond bare survival. But in his mid-twenties, Whitman undertook those burdens: in 1845 he moved nearby, then back into his parents' home, often sharing a room with his retarded younger brother. Subsequently, he relocated the family several times, finally buying a house for his mother on Ryerson St. in May 1855, only months before his father's death and the publication of *Leaves of Grass*.

In Brooklyn, Whitman assumed the role of breadwinner and authority, supplying clothes and furnishings, and taking control over his younger siblings. Besides occasional jobs as a printer or journalist, he opened an odds and ends shop in the house, later managing the family's carpentering and contracting business. In that role, he bought and sold houses, arranged mortgages and loans, and controlled the operation's finances. Thus he apparently usurped his father's position and power, doing so for the benefit and in the spirit of his mother—so strengthening not only his ties to her but also a lifelong compulsion to see his brothers and sisters as his own children. This drive toward absorption and inclusion— later central to both his beliefs and literary strategies—was evident, as Justin Kaplan points out, even in his effort to have the entire family buried in the Camden, N.J., mausoleum constructed for himself and bearing *his* name alone.

No doubt the approach of the Civil War and his party's waffling on the fugitive slave issue helped drive Whitman from politics and toward religion or poetry. But we should overlook neither the pressures of his approaching middle age nor the fuller acceptance of his sexuality, which apparently followed his 1848 sojourn in New Orleans. Clearly, New Orleans and the South always connoted a freer and more sensuous eroticism to him and, from this time onward, his view of "manly love" assumed a more cheerful and confident tone.

After his return North, recognizing that his idealistic sexual and social views forbade any future in politics and that his approaching thirtieth year demanded that he fix upon a life's work, Whitman was torn between becoming an itinerant lecturer-prophet or a poet. Fortunately, he decided to let his book do the traveling and preaching. That, of course, is the second of the choices so pivotal to his future. Despite the Romantic image of poet as seer and visionary, his choice would seem, in view of the weakness of his earlier writings, a scarcely promising decision. Influenced by the English moralistic writers Samuel Warren (*The Lily and the Bee*) and Martin Farquhar Tupper (*Proverbial Philosophy*), he set out to create a "new Bible" which would incline his countrymen, through "manly love," toward a more secure Union. Thus, he could channel drives which might endanger him and may already have brought humiliation and exclusion, transforming them into an aesthetic philosophy of acceptance and joinder.

Whitman's doctrine seems directly at odds with the facts of his life. Once returned, he remained with his family for seventeen years. True, he apparently spent most evenings in Manhattan at concerts, plays, lectures, or other social or cultural events and, probably, homosexual cruising. Only by the broadest symbolic leap can this be reckoned a "song of the open road." Yet it was here that he was able to evolve and transform personal sexual and affectional drives into an aesthetic philosophy of exploration, expansion and incorporation.

Let me stress that Whitman's doctrine—in sexual terms, this promiscuity—accepts a spiritual and imaginary interpretation almost as readily as a physical one. If many dedicated readers long ignored the basic sexual impulse of Whitman's work, that no doubt reflects a reluctance to recognize those preferences; it also reflects his deliberate ambiguity about what is intended by such terms as "manly love" or (borrowed from phrenology) "adhesiveness." For instance, section 11 of "Song of Myself" depicts a richly dressed woman hiding behind her window blinds while imagining sexual play with a band of young men swimming in the river below—obviously a symbol of the poet's relation to his world. While Robert K. Martin sees this as a plea for anonymous and promiscuous sexual experience, it may quite as well represent *imaginary* exploration and accretion. The lady delights only in peeking and fantasizing; no further action is either described or prescribed.

Whitman announces his program in passage after passage of *Leaves of Grass* (unless otherwise noted, all quotations come from the 1855 edition):

> There was a child went forth every day,
> And the first object he looked upon and received with
>   wonder of pity or love or dread, that object he became,
> And that object became part of him for the day or a
>   certain part . . . or for many years or stretching cycles
>   of years.

Such transformation and identification carries on into adult life:

> I do not ask the wounded person how he feels . . . I
>   myself become the wounded person,
> My hurt turns livid upon me as I lean on a cane and
>   observe.

This incorporation is often imaged as a love relationship ("I have embraced you, and henceforth possess you to myself"), but it may also be sublimated as the rescue of one dying or in despair. In his later life, the same urge is reenacted in Whitman's care for wounded Civil War soldiers.

Throughout Whitman's poems, a related ambiguity is found in the many passages which, taken alone, could be taken for straightforward sexual come-ons, but in context may seem invitations to a physical and/or spiritual journey. Again and again, Whitman was deliberately vague about what we should take literally, what symbolically:

> Come closer to me,
> Push close my lovers and take the best I possess
> —canceled lines from 1855, later part of
> "A Song for Occupations"

> Whoever you are holding me now in hand, . . .
> Here to put your lips upon mine I permit you,
> Or if you will, thrusting me beneath your clothing,
> Where I may feel the throbs of your heart or rest upon
> your hip,
> Carry me when you go forth over land or sea;
> —"Whoever You Are Holding Me Now
> in Hand"

> Camerado, I give you my hand!
> I give you my love more precious than money . . .
> Will you give me yourself? will you come travel with me?
> Shall we stick by each other as long as we live?
> —"Song of the Open Road"

> Out of the rolling ocean the crowd came a drop gently to me,
> Whispering
> *I love you, before long I die* . . .
> O camerado close! O you and me at last, and us two
> only/. . .
> O hand in hand! . . . O one more desirer and lover!
> —"Starting from Paumanok"

This sublimation, then, justifies and ennobles the drive for promiscuity, seeing it as a journeying toward development and expansion of the self. Many of the young men whose names Whitman collected did work as travelers—drovers, carters, sailors, streetcar drivers, ferry pilots. It is, of course, common to feel liberated, sexually or otherwise, when away from one's home; an escape from the parental world of fixed abodes, obligations, affectional restrictions and social conventions may indeed lead to far-reaching spiritual freedoms.

Obviously, neither promiscuity nor the urge to incorporate one's love objects into the self is confined to homosexuals. The lyrics of many heterosexual poets (as also our divorce rates) reveal a like urge to contain and define those we love. Still, there is probably no poet who took so literally or extensively as did Whitman the notion that lovers may and should become One.

This drive for assimilation is best integrated with Whitman's overall thought as a consolation for separation at birth from the mother—substituting for that primal joinder either a sexual unity or a loverlike inclusion in some social, political, or religious group. The first "Inscription" to the final *Leaves of Grass* opens:

> One's self I sing, a simple separate person,
> Yet utter the word Democratic, the word En-Masse.

The threatening word "separate" is immediately disarmed by the enclosing, politically maternal "Democratic." Again, in "Out of the Cradle Endlessly Rocking," the loss of a lover leads directly to a longing for return in death to the oceanic mother.

The inclusive ego, of course, may have less admirable aspects. Paul Zweig quotes a suggestive statement by Whitman: "What is it to own anything?—it is to incorporate it into yourself as the primal god swallowed the immortal offspring of Rhea and accumulated to his life and knowledge and strength all that would have grown in them." We *do* admire Whitman's appetite, his urge to ingest vast areas of divergence. Yet there remains a question whether, so incorporated, human difference has been preserved or merely homogenized and obliterated. We know that Whitman's siblings found his authority "excessive"; some of them preferred to be buried separately, under their own names. We should note Whitman's devastation when others declined to be appropriated, and his own occasional reluctance to be ingested. We should admit that sexual equalities, like political ones, can impose a shared insignificance, that most promises of universal love and comradeship have led to spiritual cannibalism.

Critics often praise or reject Whitman's doctrines accordingly as they share his opinions and/or sexual preferences. I am not questioning here the intrinsic worth of those doctrines, but rather their value to Whitman's life and work. In politics and religion— those areas Whitman most hoped to affect—they were clearly useless. The mere need for euphemisms and circumlocutions betrays that such a program would scarcely be widely accepted. Homophobia was, if anything, spreading during Whitman's lifetime; few, indeed, would have traded their communion wafer for those "baskets covered with white towels bulging the house with their plenty" offered by the visits of Whitman's fiercely erotic god.

Neither would acceptance of "comradely love" stem the nation's rush toward civil war or toward conquest. If Americans were inclined to exploration and assimilation, that was materialistic and industrial, leading not to spiritual but to material and commercial expansion, to dominance in world affairs. Neither did utopian projections quiet for long Whitman's personal distress. As his family continued its dreary slide into poverty, drunkenness, madness and abuse, his own affectional life remained tormented; despairs soon dogged him again. His notebooks are filled with the struggle to relinquish those who rejected his advances or proved unfaithful; at one time, indeed, he was prepared to give up poetry to please his lover. The "love of dear comrades" could, like any other, lead to betrayal and, finally, to a deeper loneliness.

Whitman's doctrines had already demanded extensive denials and evasions: the reinvention of his saintly mother, of his family's situation, of his own health and affectional nature. In time, he would have to assert that the Civil War was not really catastrophic, that Lincoln's assassination had been a sacrifice which saved the nation, that the United States could really be a force for spiritual brotherhood in the world. In short, Whitman could maintain his self-confident and cheerful beliefs, but only by shutting out a broader and broader awareness of the reality around him. Yet those ideas were indispensable, admitting him to wider acceptances (first of all, self-acceptance), to wider ranges of experience and discourse than any writer of his time. That preeminence was found, of course, only in areas he sometimes dismissed as "merely literary."

II. Structure

Whitman's definition of the self, with its demand for exploration and inclusion, led not only to political and religious doctrines but also, triumphantly, to his literary methods—his characteristic poetic structure; his blend of conventions, genres, and points of view, his subject matter, vocabulary and levels of language; his eccentric syntax; his prosodic and rhythmic practices. "Song of Myself" is, I think, the most powerful and ambitious poetic account of our world's nature, of our spiritual reality, since *Paradise Lost*. Yet those two poems' structural designs are diametrically opposed.

Milton—in sexual, political and literary matters vehemently judgmental and restrictive—builds his epic by definition, by exclusion, by progressive constriction. *Paradise Lost* begins with cosmic scenes of revolt and conspiracy in Hell, of warfare and of God's universal judgment in Heaven. Then the poem begins to narrow its focus, following Satan's flight through the Abyss to earth and Raphael's errand to warn Adam of the world's moral nature. The climax is reached with Eve's temptation and Adam's fall in Book IX. In the Garden of Eden all that is universal and abstract finds personal embodiment and concretion: the vast forces of Good and Evil wage their warfare in the confines of two human souls. Throughout, as E. M. W. Tillyard demonstrated, the same compulsion to define and delimit characterizes Milton's small-scale effects and local style, his constant effort to contain all reality in some one defining statement.

Whitman, per contra, the most inclusive of poets (implicitly, the most promiscuous of lovers), builds his text through expansion and inclusion. For him, the self is the ultimate definer and authority, yet only as that self can be the epitome, the container of all. Whitman depicts himself as "a fluid and swallowing character" or, later, one to "fly the flight of the fluid and swallowing soul." "Song of Myself" builds outward from the single self of the early stanzas to incorporate first the continent, next the globe, then the galactic "orchards of spheres" and finally even the abstract entities. The poem's climactic crisis lies in the effort to include death—that which appears to mandate the self's obliteration.

Milton stands for belief and hierarchy; Whitman for fact and, if not equality, a random diversity. For Milton the Tree of Knowledge equals sin, since every new bit of information may challenge his interpretation of the world's hierarchy. For Whitman, knowledge—including carnal knowledge—means salvation; the self can be nurtured only by experience. For Milton, one need know only the scene in the Garden of Eden; its interpretation explains all human existence. For Whitman, each fact and event has a separate identity and can be made One not by reason but only in the ecstasy of the lover-divinity's visits.

As noted, Whitman meant to create a new sacred text, a Bible for democracy. At one point he intended 365 poems; "Song of Myself" still falls into 52 sections. For myself, the overall structure falls into seven main divisions:

   I. Introduction to Doctrine (1–7)
  II. Expansion Through Exploration (8–23)
 III. Return to the Individual (24)
 IV. Expansion of Sense Experience (25–31)
  V. Expansion Through Species, Abstract Entities,
      into Suffering and Death (32–36)
 VI. Restoration of Faith (37–51)
VII. Acceptance of Death (52)

We set off on an overarching journey outward from the self through the continent, broken first at my division III by the protagonist's return to find that the self has now *become* a landscape or continent. After still wider and more abstract explorations, the journey is interrupted again at division V by the recognition of death and of the self's possible dissolution. This is countered in division VI by reassuring iterations of belief and, finally, in VII, the acceptance of death.

Tracing out this journey in closer detail, the poem opens with a deliberate parody of the classical epics—singing neither "The wrath of Achilles" nor "Arms and the man" but, impudently, "I celebrate myself and sing myself," then, mocking the biblical family tree of "begats," stating the poet's qualifications to be Epic Bard of Democracy:

> My tongue, every atom of my blood, form'd from this
> soil, this air,
> Born here of parents born here from parents the same,
> and their parents the same,
> I, now thirty-seven years old in perfect health begin . . .
> —lines added for the 1881 edition

Immediately, however, section 2 asserts the self's need for inclusion:

> Houses and rooms are full of perfumes . . .
> The atmosphere is not a perfume . . .
> It is for my mouth forever, I am in love with it . . .

In section 3 we achieve the first mystical union with divinity, a lover bestowing abundance and nourishment:

> As God comes a loving bedfellow and sleeps at my side
> all night and close on the peep of the day,
> And leaves me baskets covered with white towels
> bulging the house with their plenty.

Section 5 (though this is somewhat subdued in later editions) vividly describes this erotic coupling. Again, the lover-divinity imparts riches, now metaphysical, joining the poet to all physical existence:

> I mind how once we lay in June, such a transparent
> summer morning,

You settled your head athwart my hips and gently turn'd
　　over upon me,
And parted the shirt from my bosom-bone, and plunged
　　your tongue to my bare-stript heart,
And reach'd till you felt my beard, and reach'd till you
　　held my feet.

Swiftly arose and spread around me the peace and joy
　　and knowledge that pass all the art and argument of
　　the earth;
And I know that the hand of God is the elderhand of my
　　own,
And I know that the spirit of God is the eldest brother of
　　my own . . .
And limitless are leaves stiff and drooping in the fields,
And brown ants in the little wells beneath them,
And mossy scabs of the wormfence, and heaped stones,
　　and elder and mullen and pokeweed.

This leads in section 6 to a first credo, the poet's inspired hunches about the central symbol, the grass, then in section 7 to a reaffirming gospel of the self as lover of all and sundry.

After his deployment of supporting beliefs, the poet begins his journey outward (my division II). Section 8 opens with brief scenes of birth, love, and death: the baby in its cradle, the lovers on the bushy hill, the suicide on the bloody floor. This leads into one of Whitman's most vital catalogs, a montage of snapshot-like scenes of city life and ends with a declaration of the poet's aim: "I mind them or the show or resonance of them—I come and I depart."

Section 9 offers a symbolic cameo of the poet in relation to his world: a vast wagonload of hay, living, dying and dead, into which he leaps to "roll head over heels and tangle [his] hair full of wisps." We resume our journey through the nation in section 10, observing a hunter camped in the mountains, the Yankee clipper under sail, a clam diggers' outing, the marriage of the "red girl" (almost a fertility goddess), the runaway slave (almost a Christ figure). Section 11 once more interjects a symbolic cameo: the ballad-like tale of the well-dressed lady who spies on the young men bathing in the river. As already suggested, she embodies the basic paradox of the poet's role: splashing in the water, running her hands over the young men's bodies, yet actually staying "stock still in [her] room." However passionate the poet's participation, that too may be imaginative rather than literal.

On the move again, sections 12–14 extend the poet's identity beyond his race to the Negro driver of the stone dray, then out of species to the team of horses, the yoked oxen, the wood-drake and duck, to the wild gander sending down his *Ya-honk* (an invitation fully accepted and answered only in the poem's ending, with the poet's death). We have passed from land to air, from the yoked and civilized to the free and wild; the promiscuity of these loves, these identities, is acknowledged, even acclaimed, at the end of section 14:

> What is commonest, cheapest, nearest, easiest, is Me,
> Me going in for my chances, spending for vast returns,
> Adorning myself to bestow myself on the first that will
>   take me,
> Not asking the sky to come down to my good will,
> Scattering it freely forever.

Section 15, one of Whitman's finest achievements, is a panoramic catalog of the continent, each person at their characteristic occupation or activity. Moving from the northeastern scenes familiar to Whitman, place names grow steadily stranger and more distant: "Yankee . . . Missourian . . . the Red River . . . the Tennessee . . . the Arkansas . . . the Chattahoochee or Altamahaw." Simultaneously, the cycle of seasonal growth is invoked, paralleled with cycles of age and of generations. Then, in one of poetry's deftest transformations, Whitman lights the lamps and "torches shin[ing] in the dark," putting the whole continent with its inhabitants to sleep at once, then affirming his and his poem's identity with all:

> In walls of adobe, in canvas tents, rest hunters and
>   trappers after their day's sport,

> The city sleeps and the country sleeps,
> The living sleep for their time, the dead sleep for their
>   time.
> The old husband sleeps by his wife and the young
>   husband sleeps by his wife,
> And these tend inward to me, and I tend outward to them,
> And such as it is to be of these more or less I am,
> And of these one and all I weave the song of myself.
>   —last line added for 1881 edition

After further amplification of the idea of inclusion, the journey resumes in sections 21–22, realizing in passages of greatest passion the poet-lover's copulation and union with Night, Earth and the Sea.

Section 24 marks a new break (my division III) in the poem's progression. Having explored and imaginatively encompassed the continent, the poet turns inward to his private self, only to find he has become a landscape, even a continent:

> Walt Whitman, an American, one of the roughs, a kosmos,
>   . . .
> If I worship any particular thing it shall be some of the
>   spread of my body . . .
> Shaded ledges and rests, firm masculine coulter, it shall
>   be you . . .
> Root of washed sweet-flag, timorous pond-snipe, nest of
>   guarded duplicate eggs, it shall be you,
> Mixed tussled hay of head and beard and brawn it shall
>   be you . . .
> You sweaty brooks and dews it shall be you,
> Winds whose soft-tickling genitals rub against me, it shall
>   be you,
> Broad muscular fields, branches of liveoak, loving
>   lounger in my winding paths, it shall be you,
> Hands I have taken, face I have kissed, mortal I have ever
>   touched, it shall be you.

We have lost all distinction between a passionate autoeroticism ("I dote on myself . . .") and a love of others, of a world of eroticized experience:

> Hefts of the moving world at innocent gambols silently
> rising . . .
> Something I cannot see puts upward libidinous prongs,
> Seas of bright juice suffuse heaven.

With section 25 (division IV), then, the poet ventures forth again. The aim now is not so much exploration of the world as of the senses which experience it, reveling in turn (sections 28–29) in sight, speech, hearing and, climactically, touch. Those faculties have become so acutely attuned that simply to "touch my person to some one else's" leads to a scene of hectic sexual violence:

> They have left me helpless to a red marauder . . .
> You villain touch! what are you doing? my breath in its
> throat,
> Unclench your floodgates, you are too much for me.

Despite its care for detail, this passage and others like it still provoke disagreement as to exactly what is depicted; we can specify neither the participants' sex nor their actions. Harold Bloom sees this as a scene of masturbation; Michael Moon, as one of self-dismemberment; I see it as a gang rape. All these views—and others—may be partially correct. Jimmie Killingsworth justly notes that Whitman often conflates details from diverse scenes of illicit or violent sex. This may intend to avoid censorship or may merely represent how Whitman thought about such matters—showing another aspect of inclusion. The crux is that this sexual license, even violation, leads again to satisfaction and fulfillment:

> Rich showering rain, and recompense richer afterward . . .
> Sprouts take and accumulate . . . stand by the curb prolific
> and vital,
> Landscapes projected masculine full-sized and golden.

This orgasmic fulfillment provokes a new, surer and greater credo: "I believe a leaf of grass is no less than the journeywork of the stars. . . ."

Section 32 (my division V) resumes the earlier outward exploration and expansion, but with an aim even less geographical. We are concerned now with expansion through living forms and species, then through abstract entities such as Time and Space. Climactically, in a new catalog (section 33) we venture upon identity with suffering—with shipwreck victims, martyrs, a hunted slave, a wounded fireman, a dying general, and finally, in two of Whitman's finest scenes, the slaughter of 150 Texas Rangers, then the sea battle of John Paul Jones (sections 34–36).

The dramatic realization of those scenes, though triumphant, may be a Pyrrhic victory; they bring the poet only too successfully to "embody all presences outlaw'd or suffering." Though he may summon help, "You laggards there on guard! look to your arms," and try to deliver himself, "Enough! enough! enough . . . I discover myself on the verge of a usual mistake," and may even claim to rescue others—

> You there, impotent, loose in the knees,
> Open your scarf'd chops till I blow grit within you . . .
> Spread your palms and lift the flaps of your pockets . . .
> I have stores plenty and to spare . . .
>
> I seize the descending man and raise him with resistless
>   will,
> O despairer, here is my neck . . .
> Every room of the house do I fill with an arm'd force,

—this brush with death will not be securely shaken off until the poem's end.

The doctrinal aids Whitman calls up in my division VI (sections 40 through 49) seem to me only marginally successful as poetry; embodied so brilliantly at the outset, their restatement here pales in comparison. Perhaps the tenets have worn thin with reiteration; perhaps it is only that Death is a more formidable adversary. In any case, despite occasional brilliancies, this remains for me the poem's least compelling area. The doubts and terrors are eventually overcome, though not through any new approach or deeper perception; the fear itself may have partially dissipated just by being brought into the open. Clearly, Whitman evinces and embodies his victory over fear by discovering the requisite poetic image: death as a midwife or a restored mother. By section 49 a fully confident voice, and vital use of language, have reemerged:

> To his work without flinching the accoucheur comes,
> I see the elderhand pressing receiving supporting,
> I recline by the sills of the exquisite flexible doors . . . and
> mark the outlet, and mark the relief and escape . . .
>
> Of the turbid pool that lies in the autumn forest,
> Of the moon that descends the steeps of the soughing
> twilight,
> Toss, sparkles of day and dusk . . . toss on the black stems
> that decay in the muck,
> Toss to the moaning gibberish of the dry limbs.
>
> I ascend from the moon . . . I ascend from the night,
> And perceive of the ghastly glitter the sunbeams
> reflected,
> And debouch to the steady and central from the offspring
> great or small.

This image of death as rebirth leads on to the final section's exultant tone and inventive vigor. Here, the poet does answer the earlier call of the spotted hawk, does cheerfully view his own death and dissolution:

> The last scud of day holds back for me,
> It flings my likeness after the rest and true as any on the
> shadowed wilds,
> It coaxes me to the vapor and the dusk.

As in "Out of the Cradle Endlessly Rocking," the image of death returns us to the mother. In that later, despairing poem of lost love, death provides merely relief, the comfort and respite of the womb; here, in Whitman's determinedly optimistic epic, death leads to rebirth, to renewed growth "from the grass I love," and to the jauntiness of "If you want me again look for me under your bootsoles." That, in turn, leads the poet to one final, flirtatious lover's invitation:

> Failing to fetch me at first keep encouraged,
> Missing me one place search another,
> I stop some where waiting for you.

III. SYNERGY AND SYNTACTICS

Ralph Waldo Emerson described *Leaves of Grass* as "a combination of the *Baghavat-Gita* and the *New York Herald*." Charles Eliot Norton wrote of "this gross yet elevated, this superficial yet profound, this preposterous yet somehow fascinating book . . . [a] mixture of Yankee transcendentalism and New York rowdyism." Richard Chase called "Song of Myself" an "extraordinary collection of small imagist poems, versified short stories, realistic urban and rural genre paintings, inventories, homilies, philosophizings, farcical episodes, confessions and lyric musings," which promised "along with ecstasy, pain and surreal journeyings, a strange admixtue of wit, humor, clowning, comic boasting, Western brag, Yankee laconism, conscious absurdity and colossal egotism."

Is this applause or jeering? It sounds almost like Polonius's "tragedy, comedy, history, pastoral, pastoral-comical, historical-pastoral, tragical historical, tragical-comical-historical-pastoral; scene individable, or poem unlimited." Of course, Shakespeare himself had been criticized for mixing tragedy with comedy, verse with prose, high language with low, history with myth. Assimiliation of various genres, modes and styles was a crucial strategy for

Whitman. His hero is not the extraordinary man who performs some remarkable act—conquers a city, invents a machine, commits a terrible crime—but the common man who daily constructs a self from the particulars of experience. That implies not only the facts of our physical cosmos, but also the ways that others experience those facts and then embody those awarenesses in diverse linguistic forms; our story contains not only others' stories, but also the manner of their renderings. Just so, the way that Whitman tells the story of democracy, of the common man, the loving "comrade" and "elève" carries much of his meaning.

Such critics as Gay Wilson Allen have related Whitman's encompassing and "expanding ego" to his use of verse catalogs; others have pointed out those catalogs' role in the "democratic" subversion of social distinctions, of authority and subordination. William Gass writes, "Lists suppress the verb . . . since the command itself is never set down, the list feigns passivity and politeness . . . [Lists] . . . tend to confer equality on their members." Not only do Whitman's enumerations flaunt improprieties—facts and details unmentionable to others—but these are enjambed with the most "elevated" aspects of the society. Thus, his best catalogs are not only "democratic," but vivid and startling throughout. Section 15 is rife with examples:

> The prostitute draggles her shawl, her bonnet bobs on her
>   tipsy and pimpled neck,
> The crowd laugh at her blackguard oaths, the men jeer
>   and wink at each other,
> (Miserable! I do not laugh at your oaths nor jeer you,)
> The President holds a cabinet council, he is surrounded
>   by the great secretaries,
> On the piazza walk five friendly matrons with twined
>   arms;
> The crew of the fish-smack pack repeated layers of
>   halibut in the hold,

Readers unfamiliar with the literary atmosphere of the 1850s and 1860s may miss the breaches of decorum here. Other poets might have mentioned a prostitute; none would have evinced any close interest in her neck. Still others might have mentioned halibut; none would have brought it into close company with society matrons. Yet if readers were shocked by such questions of literary style, greater outrage, more violent rejections would have risen from recognition of their origin and symbology in the advocacy of "adhesion" or promiscuous sexual contact—from Whitman's deeper aim, admission of his sexual tendencies into "polite" society. "Shut not your doors to me" is his demand not only of "proud libraries."

The "democracy" of Whitman's intent is equally heard in his word choice and levels of language. His most vivid passages often depend on slang and / or new coinages: "The blab of the pave, . . . the sluff of bootsoles . . . [the butcher boy's] repartee and his shuffle and breakdown . . . Shoulder your duds, dear son . . . a poke-easy from sandhills and pines . . . life is a suck and a sell . . . [w]ashes and razors for foofoos . . . [h]efts of the moving world . . ."etc. On the other hand, his language can be surprisingly literary—least successfully so when he lards a passage with French or high-toned phrases meant to "dignify" his doctrine. His voice is most vital when slang collides with other speech levels, often enough with highly literary lines:

> Our foe was no skulk in his ship, I tell you,
> His was the surly English pluck, and there is no tougher
>   and truer, and never was and never will be;
> Along the lowered eve he came, horribly raking us.
>   —the word "surly" added in 1867

The third line—literary, almost "poetical"—sharply counters the old salt's language with an echo of the romanticized adventure tales then familiar to most readers.

Among Whitman's fractures of customary usage, we might specify his use of parentheses. Often, as Jean Catel suggests, this signals a shift of voice or gesture breaking the level of discourse, though at times it may indicate only an inserted stage direction: "The regatta is spread on the bay, the race is begun, (how the white sails sparkle!)" Elsewhere, just as a painter might break through his own picture plane, Whitman may interrupt his scene to comment to the reader: "The young fellow drives the express-wagon, (I love him though I do not know him.)" or even to address the characters, "(Miserable! I do not laugh at your oaths or jeer you.)" Elsewhere, other interjections which seem equally parenthetical—"You should have been with us that day round the chowder-kettle"—have no parentheses. Indeed, Whitman seems at times to use parentheses to assert his freedom to be inconsistent as one aspect of inclusiveness: "Do I contradict myself? / Very well then I contradict myself, / (I am large, I contain multitudes.)"

Whitman is often most inventive when he wants his message or subject not too fully understood and so leaves open multiple interpretations—as we noted earlier of sections 28–29. One of the most striking passages comes from the 1855 version of "The Sleepers" which, later deleted, was long available only in quotations by such French critics as Catel.

> I feel ashamed to go naked about the world,
> And am curious to know where my feet stand . . . and
>   what is this flooding me, childhood or manhood . . .
>   and the hunger that crosses the bridge between.
>
> The cloth laps a first sweet eating and drinking,
> Laps life-swelling yolks . . . laps ears of rose-corn, milky
>   and just ripened:
> The white teeth stay, and the boss-tooth advances in
>   darkness,
> And liquor is spilled on lips and bosoms by touching
>   glasses, and the best liquor afterward.

Recording a dream of oral intercourse through substituted symbolic objects and actions, thus leaping nearly into the surreal, the passage is stylistically unparalleled in his work.

Whitman also reappropriates linguistic forms, frequently interchanging parts of speech, so denying society's rules for parts of speech, as elsewhere of the body. That, too, may have lost effect for readers familiar with later poets who've followed Whitman's example. For later writers, however, such substitutions often provide no more than a spice to liven the poem's texture, not, as for

Whitman, conveying basic qualities of mind and personality.

Although he may occasionally coin a verb from another part of speech, Whitman most characteristically creates nouns from verbs or adjectives: "Dash me with amorous wet" ... "What blurt is this ... life is a suck and a sell ... I snuff the sidle of evening ... the vitreous pour of the full moon ... rock me in billowy drowse." In a phrase like "[t]he blab of the pave," *two* verbs have become nouns. This inclination is closely involved with the penchant for catalogs and lists, for indiscriminated collections of objects. Such "democratic" forms help present a world where movement, though always present, is curiously frozen into a state. Paul Elmer More, in his *Shelburne Essays* of 1922, notes a comparable effect:

> [A] sense of indiscriminate motion is ... left finally by Whitman's work ... Now the observer seems to be moving through clustered objects beheld vividly for a second of time and then lost in the mass, and, again, the observer himself is stationary while the visions throng past him in almost dizzy rapidity; but in either case we come away with the feeling of having been merged in unbroken processions, whose beginning and end are below the distant horizon, and whose meaning we but faintly surmise.

This effect is embodied not only in catalogs and in the forming of nouns of action but also in Whitman's peculiar syntax. This turns many a long sentence into a catalog of clauses and phrases, subverting the normal English sentence with its defined subordinations, action and sense of forward thrust. Instead, Whitman uses fragments or ambiguous structures, hiding the primary subject and verb amid strings of moderative phrases, gerundive or participial forms, even using misleading punctuation to disguise the supposed main actor and action.

We often use such ambiguous constructions in conversation where facial expressions, vocal intonations and bodily stance help to clarify our meaning. Taken over as a literary device, such a syntax contributes much to More's "sense of indiscriminate motion," of being "merged in unbroken processions." Since the usual subordinations and the sense of directed motion have been unstrung, we move through the sentence tentatively, trying alternate interpretations, held in a kind of stasis and passivity. Everything is *depicted* in the process of happening; nothing happens. Consider the first poem from *Children of Adam*:

TO THE GARDEN THE WORLD

> To the garden the world anew ascending,
> Potent mates, daughters, sons, preluding,
> The love, the life of their bodies, meaning and being,
> Curious here behold my resurrection after slumber,
> The revolving cycles in their wide sweep having brought
>   me again,
> Amorous, mature, all beautiful to me, all wondrous,
> My limbs and the quivering fire that ever plays through
>   them, for reasons, most wondrous,
> Existing I peer and penetrate still,
> Content with the present, content with the past,
> By my side or back of me Eve following,
> Or in front, and I following her just the same.

We do not reach the subject and main verb, do not know who speaks, who takes what action, until the eighth of these eleven lines. Even punctuation, or its absence, obscures the putative subject and predicate. Moreover, the chief actor and his acts—"I peer and penetrate still"—interest us less than do the preceding phrases which pretend to modify them but which actually depict a reawakening to the world's sexual cycles—not exactly a secondary or subordinate matter. We sense a mind more compelled by the journey's experience than by any purported destination.

If we rearranged these lines into conventional English, making clear the main syntactic structure, we would come up with at least three sentences:

> I curiously behold my resurrection after slumber:
> My limbs and the quivering fire that ever plays through
>   them
> Ascending for reasons most wondrous to the garden, the
>   world,
> All beautiful, all wondrous.
> Since the revolving cycles in their wide sweep have
>   brought me here again,
> Amorous, mature, I still peer and penetrate,
> Existing and content with the present, content with the
>   past.
> Eve follows by my side or in back of me,
> Or in front, and I follow her just the same,
> A prelude to potent mates, daughters, sons,
> Since we mean and are the love and the life of their bodies.

That seems dull enough for most literary magazines – announcing a meaning but enacting none. True, it's easier to understand: there's less to be understood. By clarifying the "perverse" dislocations and disjunctions, replacing the gerunds and participles with active verbs, I've dispelled the air of suspension and ambiguity—and, thereby, the unfakeable part of Whitman's meaning.

In the original, is the speaker (Adam or his newly reborn representative, the poet-father-teacher) the prelude to potent mates, daughters, and sons? Or are those mates, daughters, and sons themselves a prelude to others? Is it Adam, Eve or those mates and offspring who is / are amorous, mature, beauteous, and wondrous, who provide "meaning and being"? The answer to all such questions is, "Yes." Syntactic reciprocity is precisely the point; all elements interact as mutual causes and effects. We have a grammatical daisy-chain where almost every phrase can interact and form a temporary copula with every other. Only one mind could have produced this passage; any university committee or free love society could have written mine.

We find a similar strategy in the fifty-seven lines of the cycle's next poem, "From Pent-Up Aching Rivers." Here again prepositional phrases, gerunds, participles, and parentheses (some, complete sentences) hold us in suspense; the main subject and verb appear only in lines 55 and 56:

> From the hour of shining stars and dropping dews,
> From the night a moment I emerging flitting out,
> Celebrate you act divine and you children prepared for,
> And you stalwart loins.

Or, once more, the magnificent verse paragraph that opens "Out of the Cradle"; the subject appears only in the twentieth of its twenty-two lines. The main verb—in an inversion which would have startled even Milton—is displaced to the paragraph's very last word.

> Throwing myself on the sand, confronting the waves,
> I, chanter of pains and joys, uniter of here and hereafter,
> Taking all hints to use them, but swiftly leaping beyond
> them,
> A reminiscence sing.

Perhaps the ultimate use of such techniques comes in section 36 of "Song of Myself," which describes the *Bonhomme Richard* and the *Serapis* devastated after their battle. Though the first line, "Stretch'd and still lies the midnight," might be a complete, though inverted sentence, we proceed at once to noun phrases, gerunds and participles, the fragments and loose structures which bring the scene to a deathly stasis into which are suddenly projected the horror of the surgery and the narrator's appalled exclamation:

> Delicate sniffs of sea-breeze, smells of sedgy grass and
> fields by the shore, death-messages given in charge to
> survivors,
> The hiss of the surgeon's knife, the gnawing teeth of his
> saw,
> Wheeze, cluck, swash of falling blood, short wild scream,
> and long, dull, tapering groan,
> These so, these irretrievable.

For this astonishing climax, Whitman again transforms onomato-poeic verbs into the fixity of nouns, "Wheeze, cluck, swash of falling blood," so injecting a moment of irretrievable tragedy. Significantly, this comes just at the point in "Song of Myself" where Whitman, almost overcome by his identification with suffering and death, is cast into doubt and near despair.

IV. LINE AND RHYTHM

The use a poet makes of literary conventions commonly reflects a response to broader social and cultural traditions. When using traditional forms, some are satisfied merely to fill out a metrical paradigm; those more resistant or eccentric will bend those patterns into their own modes of thought and voice. Milton, using theoreti-cal contractions,"elisions," partly derived from Puritan psalmody, could justify up to fifteen syllables in a line supposedly limited to ten. John Donne's satires wrenched the accent patterns so violently that Alexander Pope (moved, perhaps, in an age obsessed with minor perfections of form, by his own physical disfigurement) revised and "versified" those satires into propriety. Whitman's case, given the ineptitude of his early poems in traditional forms, was more drastic; wrenching the conventions would scarcely suffice. He could no more adapt to his society's literary practices than to its mating rituals—to strict couplets, if you will. To realize his mind's musics, Whitman had to invent new tactics, artifices, usages, link-ages, devising what we might call a polymorphous per-Verse.

When discussing metrical work, we usually focus on the range of variations in a poetic line: number and position of accents and / or light syllables, long and/or short syllables; the occurrence of caesuras, rhyme, alliteration, or other sound devices; coincidence of poetic lines with sentence structures. Whitman's methods turn his attention to a broader question: how could lines of random lengths and movements—which might have come from one of the traditional forms or from *none*—coexist in a larger unity? The problem is directly parallel to those he addressed in politics and religion: not to discard earlier beliefs, but to incorporate them into a more encompassing, democratic system. His aim is not to prescribe a doctrine, a social manner, a metrical system that will control all subgroups and subsystems but, rather, to find ways for the full diversity to cohabit.

From time to time, Whitman wrote lines with little rhythmical definition or musical surcharge, lines that look and sound like prose:

> Do you think matter has cohered together from its
>   diffused float, and the soil is on the surface and water
>   runs and vegetation sprouts for you . . . and not for
>   him and her?
>   —"I Sing the Body Electric"

> O the strange fascination of these half-known, half-
>   impassable swamps, infested by reptiles, resounding
>   with the bellow of the alligator, the sad noises of the
>   night-owl and the wild-cat, and the whirr of the
>   rattlesnake . . .
>   —"O Magnet South"

> Stately, solemn, withdrawn, baffled, mad, turbulent,
>   feeble, dissatisfied,
> Desperate, proud, fond, sick, accepted by men, rejected
>   by men . . .
>   —"Song of the Open Road"

That these longer lines should sound like prose is no mere coincidence. In English, shorter lines tend toward a musical rhythm and shape. In lines that grow beyond, say, five stresses, patterning of accents and rhythm is likely to break down. It's no accident, either, that the prosier lines often embody catalogs; Whitman's passion for incorporation reaches beyond attitudes and objects to styles and manners of movement—including that of prose.

Though most readers expect such prosey lines and consider them characteristic, fewer note how often Whitman uses traditional modes. Lois Ware notes that he "exemplified . . . at some point or other virtually all of the conventions that he professed to eschew, and that he employed some of these conventions on a large scale." Using traditional modes at will, Whitman feels no commitment, however, to continue or develop them. Many poems open with a line that, by itself, implies a conventional norm. This rises partly from the natural rhythms of English but must also reflect Whitman's wide reading of metrical poets. Iambic pentameter openings are common:

> I celebrate myself and sing myself
> Flood-tide below me! I see you face to face!
> Whoever you are holding me now in hand,
> A march in the ranks hard-prest and the road unknown

Such "iambics" resemble those of many later Romantic poets, admitting extra light syllables *ad lib* between normal accents. The first of his "Inscriptions"

> One's self I sing, a simple separate person
> Yet utter the word Democratic, the word En-Masse.

opens with a regular iambic pentameter line but so many light syllables are added in the next line that we might seem to have moved to an anapestic or an accentual norm.

Iambic or trochaic tetrameter beginnings also appear:

> Weapon, shapely, naked, wan,
> When Lilacs last in the dooryard bloomed,
> Ashes of soldiers South or North,

Iambic trimeters are most common of all:

I sing the body electric,
In cabin'd ships at sea,
O take my hand, Walt Whitman!
By blue Ontario's shore,

This preponderance becomes even more striking if we include three-stress lines which start sections or stanzas within poems.

Whitman had good reason to open with a "regular" line, so inviting readers by a suggestion that they can expect "regular" and manageable poetry—though that expectation will be dismissed, often by the very next line. More important, the short opening line allows Whitman to follow his lifelong inclination to lengthen and weight successive lines. That, of course, is one aspect of that drive toward expansion and accumulation we've been tracing.

That tendency, as critics have noted, often builds a "triangular" stanza from progressively longer lines. At the end, we sometimes find the longest line of all, but more often a shorter line or two will form, with the opening lines, a syntactic and/or rhythmic envelope:

No labor-saving machine,
No discovery have I made,
Nor will I be able to leave behind me any wealthy
     bequest to found a hospital or library,
Nor reminiscence of any deed of courage for America,
Nor literary success nor intellect, nor book for the
     bookshelf,
But a few carols vibrating through the air I leave,
For comrades and lovers.

This stanza begins with a line of three well-defined accents, moves into ambiguous longer lines, then closes with shorter lines. The last, "For comrades and lovers," with only two accents, gains finality by alliteration with "carols" and by echoing the rhythm of "nor book for the bookshelf."

A remarkable example is found at the beginning of "Song of the Broad-Axe," where the central third and fourth lines are formed by simply doubling the opening (and closing) lines:

> Weapon shapely, naked, wan,
> Head from the mother's bowels drawn,
> Wooded flesh and metal bone, limb only one and lip only
>   one,
> Gray-blue leaf by red-heat grown, helve produced from a
>   little seed sown,
> Resting the grass amid and upon,
> To be lean'd and to lean on.

If we were to break the two middle lines at their caesura,

> Wooded flesh and metal bone,
> Limb only one and lip only one,
> Gray-blue leaf by red-heat grown,
> Helve produced from a little seed sown,

the whole stanza would have eight quite regular lines which might be called either truncated iambics or four-foot accentual verse; moreover, we have slant rhymes throughout. We also find Whitman's usual tendency to accretion both in added light syllables and in the stress-loading of "Gray-blue leaf by red-heat grown" or in "little seed sown," which fills the place earlier taken by only two stresses. Such growth by adding ambiguous stresses is highly typical of Whitman; Sculley Bradley has termed this a "hovering accent"—a valuable notion in grasping Whitman's characteristic verse movement.

Using Bradley's scansion, we might examine "Tears," a third example of the triangulated stanza. Bradley argues not only that each of its three stanzas has its own climactic crest of growth, but that the whole poem embodies a triangle, ending with the line "Of tears! tears! tears!" forming an envelope with the nearly identical first line. Here, the first stanza will suffice:

>   /   /   /
> Tears! tears! tears!
>   /   /   /
> In the night, in solitude, tears,

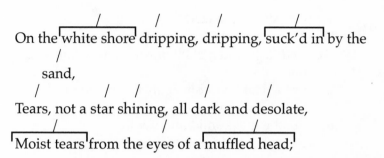

For the accent to fall on several joined stresses, or even on a short phrase, does indeed correspond to the way we read Whitman aloud. We hear not so much an irregular alternation of stressed and unstressed syllables as a current of "lifts" and "dips" similar to the movement of Anglo-Saxon alliterative meter.

From time to time, however, wanting a more defined rhythmic quality which announces itself outright as "poetry," Whitman evolved a device very much his own, though related to the freer forms sought by several late Romantic poets. Here lines are composed not of feet (though William Carlos Williams might have called them "variable feet") but, rather, of phrases—used in the grammatical sense of "meaningful units of spoken words, preceded and followed by pauses." Elsewhere I've described these passages as embodying a rhythmic theme-and-variations. The initial theme will usually have either two or three marked stresses that tend to fall equidistant in time while lighter syllables fit themselves in as they may. Such a motif may be stated either once or twice in the first line, then varied and complicated in following lines. Not only the number of syllables between stresses or of stresses in the phrase but the number of such phrases in a line may increase or decrease in the swelling or ebbing of the music's development.

The opening of "Tears, Tears, Tears," quoted above, is an obvious example. The theme, three heavily stressed syllables, is repeated in the first line; the next adds several light syllables between stresses; then later lines elaborate this basic pulse. This device turns up in work from many parts of Whitman's career, "Beat! Beat! Drums!—Blow! Bugles! Blow!" offering a further example.

The source of this form probably lies in Whitman's admiration for Tennyson's

> Break, break, break
>   On thy cold gray stones, O Sea!
> And I would that my tongue could utter
>   The thoughts that arise in me.

and for the same author's "Tears, Idle Tears." Whitman, of course, handles rhythms more broadly, more widely varying the number of stress units per line. Yet either poet could have evolved the form from the old accentual nursery rhymes, which have lines of four beats or of three beats and a rest: "Three Blind Mice" or "Hot Cross Buns."

Such a theme may be announced less conspicuously, while variations may be pursued at greater length. Among Whitman's Civil War poems is a superb small poem notable as well for brilliant camera work:

CAVALRY CROSSING A FORD

> A line in long array where they wind betwixt green
>   islands,
> They take a serpentine course, their arms flash in the
>   sun—hark to the musical clank,
> Behold the silvery river, in it the splashing horses
>   loitering stop to drink,
> Behold the brown-faced men, each group, each person a
>   picture, the negligent rest on the saddles,
> Some emerge on the opposite bank, others are just
>   entering the ford—while,
> Scarlet and blue and snowy white,
> The guidon flags flutter gaily in the wind.

Here, again, is a three-beat theme, repeated with slight additions in the second half. The next line grows to three such cadences while the body of the poem works and modulates that rhythm toward four stresses in each phrase. Specially deserving note is the way "loitering" in line three reflects, in movement, its meaning and how "while" in line five, replacing a whole three- or four-beat phrase, draws dramatic attention to what follows. The last two lines introduce a different movement to complement a new point of view. The same three-beat cadence is the basis of the splendid "Bivouac on a Mountain Side," the next poem in the book.

Whitman's most brilliant use of such variations, however, lies in the opening verse paragraph of "Out of the Cradle Endlessly Rocking":

> Out of the cradle endlessly rocking
> Out of the mocking-bird's throat, the musical shuttle,
> Out of the Ninth-month midnight,
> Out of the sterile sands and the fields beyond, where the
>   child leaving his bed wander'd alone, bareheaded,
>   barefoot,
> Down from the shower'd halo,
> Up from the mystic play of shadows twining and twisting
>   as if they were alive,
> Out from the patches of briers and blackberries,
> From the memories of the bird that chanted to me,
> From your memories sad brother, from the fitful risings
>   and fallings I heard,
> From under that yellow half-moon, late-risen and swollen
>   as if with tears,
> From those beginning notes of yearning and love there in
>   the mist,
> From the thousand responses of my heart never to cease,
> From the myriad thence-arous'd words,
> From the word stronger and more delicious than any,
> From such as now they start the scene revisiting,
> As a flock, twittering, rising, or overhead passing,
> Borne hither, ere all eludes me, hurriedly,
> A man, yet by these tears a little boy again,
> Throwing myself on the sand, confronting the waves,

I, chanter of pains and joys, uniter of here and hereafter,
Taking all hints to use them, but swiftly leaping beyond
       them,
A reminiscence sing.

Again, the basic motif—now, only two beats—is announced and
repeated in the first line, then lengthened in the second by an extra
stress in its first half. The third line picks up this three-beat variant,
while the fourth seems to have abandoned it. At once, however, the
fifth line returns to the three-beat version. Through the whole
stanza this process of variation, complication and return organizes
and vivifies the movement of the voice. Later, as one might expect
in so long and complex a composition, other devices and techniques
take over. But just when it is almost forgotten, Whitman fetches that
rhythm back for his closing:

       . . . the song of my dusky demon and brother,
       That he sang to me in the moonlight on Paumanok's gray
              beach
       With the thousand responsive songs at random,
       My own songs awaked from that hour,
       And with them the word up from the waves, the word of
              the sweetest song and of all songs,
       (Or like some old crone, rocking the cradle, swathed in
              sweet garments, bending aside,)
       The sea whispered me.

That rhythm's reprise is as hair-raising as anything in our poetry.
       The composition of "Out of the Cradle Endlessly Rocking" took
a route just the opposite to what one might expect. Rather than posit
a theme, then work variations on that, Whitman ransacked the
variations to find, late in the process, their dormant theme, the
present first line. The poem first appeared in the third (1860) edition
of *Leaves of Grass*, where it began "Out of the rock'd cradle," a line with
little musical interest or relation to the poem's later movement. That
opening remained in 1867, though in succeeding lines several varia-
tions of the (still unstated) theme first appear. That crucial motif first

is seen in a hand written, but rejected, variant for that 1867 edition, appearing in print only in 1871. The marvelous reprise came only in the seventh edition of 1881, the last before the "Deathbed" version.

Critics have often commented that as Whitman grew older he paid more attention to making his verse musical and regular. This has an element of truth and is, I think, a natural development as Whitman's beliefs became less exciting in themselves and less able to cover his experience. We might say that Whitman's early poems (like Beethoven's late work) tend to take any variation on a theme as the basis and jumping-off point for new variations; in his later work he more often returns to build variations directly from the first original theme; thus, his musical effects become more intense because less widely variant. At the same time, it must be said that in his later work he also interposes, more frequently, sharply arhythmic passages to conflict with those musics.

A good example stands at the very beginning of the 1855 "Song of Myself":

[1]

> I celebrate myself
> And what I assume you shall assume,
> For every atom belonging to me as good belongs to you.
>
> I loafe and invite my soul,
> I lean and loafe at my ease . . . observing a spear of
>   summer grass.

[2]

> Houses and rooms are full of perfumes . . . the shelves are
>   crowded with perfumes,
> I breathe the fragrance myself, and know it and like it,
> The distillation would intoxicate me also, but I shall not
>   let it.

As so often later, this version opens with a three-stress phrase:

I **celebrate** my**self**

which grows into a four-beat line, built from two-beat units:

And what **I** as**sume**   **you** shall as**sume**

then closes with a line of seven beats, divided by a caesura into four and three:

For **every atom** be**long**ing to **me**   as **good** be**longs** to **you**.

If we were to break this line at its caesura, we would have another triangulated stanza—somewhat reminiscent of the ballad stanza—having four rhythmical cadences of which the first and last echo each other's rhythms,

I celebrate myself
As good belongs to you

while the longer central cadences similarly echo each other:

And what I assume you shall assume
For every atom belonging to me

In 1855 the two-beat rhythm continues into section 2, where the internal rhymes (echoing the word "assume" in section 1) seem to imitate and mock the cloying atmosphere, the intoxication, of the scented houses:

Houses and rooms are full of perfumes . . . the shelves are
crowded with perfumes.

No doubt some poetaster of that period, intoxicated by this perfume of rhyme, might have babbled on:

Houses and rooms
Are full of perfumes;
The shelves are crowded with perfumes.
I breathe them and know
Their fragrance also;
I won't let it master me though.

Instead, Whitman gave us a line, "I breathe the fragrance myself and know it and like it," which *could* break into two such cadences. Then, drawing himself completely away from that mood, he continues with a prosey line disdainful of such rhythm and indulgence, "The distillation would intoxicate me also, but I shall not let it."

This 1855 patterning seems to offer a logical rhythmic development and a satisfactory musical texture to carry the poem. Yet in later editions Whitman makes a canny addition to the first line:

I celebrate myself and sing myself

Not only does this sharpen the mockery of the classics, but also it provides a more emphatic rhythmic base for the whole passage—a development much like what we traced in the later revisions of "Out of the Cradle." Since we now have alliterations and heavy echoes on four syllables—*cel-, -self, sing, -self*—we tend to hear only one stress in "celebrate"; stress on the third syllable fades. Further, following the natural phrasing, we are more likely to hear a stanza formed of two-beat half-lines:

I celebrate myself   and sing myself
And what I assume   you shall assume.
For every atom   belonging to me
As good belongs to you

which is capped and closed by the expected three-beat line.

Having established this more marked music, Whitman breaks it with ten arhythmic lines:

168

My tongue, every atom of my blood, formed from this
    soil, this air
Born here of parents born here from parents the same,
    and their parents the same,
I, now thirty-seven years old in perfect health begin,
Hoping to cease not till death.
Creeds and schools in abeyance,
Retiring back a while sufficed at what they are, but never
    forgotten,
I harbor for good or bad, I permit to speak at every
    hazard,
Nature without check with original energy.

When Whitman reprints the unrevised section 2, we hear in it (because of the more defined rhythm of section 1) a progression like the first section's development—two-beat phrases building into three, then into prose:

Houses and rooms   are full of perfumes
    the houses are crowded with perfumes.
I breathe the fragrance myself   and know it and like it
The distillation would intoxicate me also, but I shall not
    let it.

Thus, by adding three words in section 1, he has not only made that passage more musical, he has also made the unchanged section 2 seem more closely related in rhythm.

I have suggested, then, three germinal models to which Whitman approximates; of course, we have every manner of compound and hybrid from those models. As always, he insists on having it both ways at once. Or all ways. He can incorporate lines having no rhythmical or metrical qualities or can use any resource open to metrical verse. Beyond that, and unlike so many of those who demand freedom from rules, he managed to invent his own distinctive method and idiom, then was able to meld all these disparate kinds of verse movement, with their hybrids, into a style more capacious and generous than any one mode could provide alone.

V. Conclusions

Stephen Dunn begins a poem:

> Because the mind will defend anything
> it has found the body doing . . .

The neuroscientists Gazzaniga and LeDoux, in *The Integrated Mind*, concur:

> It is as if the verbal self looks out and sees what the person is doing, and from that knowledge it interprets [i.e., constructs] a reality.

This "verbal self," the language system centered in the brain's left hemisphere, constructs its vision of reality without full access to other areas of the brain's awareness or to the person's actual motivation. The brain, these authors demonstrate, needing to make credible its interpretations, will invent causes and motives, facts which it finds credible or convenient but which may substantially differ from what actually took place. These fictive inventions the kinder scientists refer to as "confabulations." With passing time, however, (John Jay Chapman, as I have noted elsewhere, gives us three weeks) so much new information may accumulate that the verbal self's assertions may sound like defensive rationalizations or simply lies.

We see something related in Whitman's construction of a system of ideas to justify the ways of men with men, then in its gradual decay into a defended and defensive dogma. In itself, the belief is neither more true nor false than at first, yet its telling has less and less the ring of a discovered truth about it. The self and its awareness have grown beyond beliefs it dare not surrender. We know how far Whitman's projection departed from the facts of his life—it was invented precisely for that divergence. It aimed to transform the sometimes grubby facts of his day-to-day existence into something both grand and representative, something transcendental. For all its high cost, it did just that: it helped transform him into our greatest poet.

But we might consider another quotation. Richard Chase, toward the end of his career, weary of the high-flown theorizing his researches into mythology had provoked, suggested that the best definition of a myth might be simply: a story that isn't true. Vastly different from a lie; merely being false, divergent from fact, does not prevent a story from revealing truths. How many of our acquaintances reveal themselves best in the lies they tell about themselves? Wanting to better recognize your friends, hold a masquerade: by their disguises shall ye know them. If we view Whitman's doctrine as a myth, it is indeed representative—not only does it assert a common American aspiration and a covert relation between homosexuality and democracy; it reveals, if not the facts, the qualities of Whitman's sexual life. Had he merely presented the facts—come out of the closet—it is quite possible that he could not have produced poems at all. He might well have become an outcast or derelict; in any case, he would have had no reason to invent so brilliant, but finally so revealing, an intellectual and artistic costume.

Just as the Victorians, whom we feel free to scorn, concealed their sexuality, only to find that this hidden truth soon expressed itself in every part of their lives—their language, clothing, fabrics, household furnitures—all that Hortense Calisher once called "genteel porn." So with Whitman: the facts he labored to suppress and transfigure soon seeped into every technical aspect of his work. One of the truths about Whitman was that he hid some of the truth. Is any of us so simple, so monolithic, that he or she can tell the world, flatly and beyond cavil, "This is who I am"? Is any of us so deadly dull, so brain-damaged, so deprived of the common human heritage as to have no deeps or dungeons hidden out of sight, if not out of mind? Yet how many can claim that *our* reticences, our disguises, our lies and myths have revealed so much, have produced such rich rewards?

METER, MUSIC, MEANING

I am not messing into those weary squabbles about whether poets should use traditional meters. Since neither adopting nor rejecting any system or prescription guarantees excellence, that must be hassled out between the poet and his or her poem. I *do* assume that poems have resonances which most prose hasn't; why else are they so hard to translate? Though their dictionary sense, their message content, is not to be ignored, poems draw heavily on such sub- and semiconscious factors as sound texture, suggestion and ambiguity, syntax patterns, levels of language and imagery – and on meter, rhythm and musicality, the qualities I'm investigating here. In neurological lingo, to the analysis and intellection of the brain's left hemisphere, a poem adds implication and resonance from the emotional, musical and spatial resources of the right side and from primitive internal areas. We've always said that poems offer a richer complex of thought and feeling—that is, of cortical activity.

I assume, too, that we ask an artist for something his or her own, the product of a unique mental and emotional structure. Styles, techniques, habits of composition convey the qualities of an individual sensibility, so offering readers the growth implied by projection into another's perceptions and responses, another's complex of connections. Those personal qualities, evading group beliefs and strictures, naturally tend to harbor in less conscious areas; sadly, this means that we may be less than aware of our own private characteristics. To recall this book's superscription, it *does* take most of us a long time to discover our distinctive sounds; many never do. And we are not much better at spotting the genuine in others—need I recall the 1902 roster of the greatest living poets? We are not the first age—nor, let's hope, the last—to discover that many minds, once thought inventive and original, had merely been fashionable.

Could any system tell you how to sound like yourself? That's what systems aim to modify, even squelch. Nicanor Parra proposed that we stop telling poets to conform to this doctrine or that program (artistic, philosophical, religious or political); just ask them to improve upon the blank page—i.e., upon silence. Obviously that's not accomplished by telling us things we've already heard, things some group is already jamming our ears and minds with.

My aim, then, is to ask: What use is meter? What good was it or might it be? Even when such forms were in almost universal use, critics provided little insight, seldom went beyond prescribing the "rules" for a particular form. That not only fails to guarantee beauty, *any* rule, too well obeyed, nearly guarantees the trite and dull. Indeed, such criticism led writers who had little rhythmic vitality to believe that through propriety, obedience to rules, they could rise to beauty. Nonetheless, for hundreds of years, more dynamic spirits found those forms an aid toward improving upon silence. Whether poets or leaders *consciously* grasped the how and why of their prosody's advantages, its forms helped exploit our language's rhythmic possibilities—a resource concurrent with the organic rhythms, also unconscious, which control mind and body. The sources, causes and effects of poetic meter, then, can offer promising, unexplored areas of meaning for both readers and writers.

No doubt, older methods may have to be abandoned in adjusting to changes of language or social context. I would argue only that it will not be easy to finds methods equally resonant and resourceful. As the Russian hoax poet Kozma Prutkov wrote: "Who prevents thee from inventing waterproof gunpowder?" Those poets and critics who led the attack on conventional metrics assumed that a new prosodic method would arise in its place; no such thing occurred. In the absence of any system available to our culture as a whole, only a voice as individually fertile as Walt Whitman's will suffice. As we noted earlier, when he could not produce anything remarkable in conventional meters, Whitman devised methods serviceable to (because derived from) his own qualities. The admirable in *any* field seldom ask freedom from; they take freedom for. That makes it all harder—but don't we ask artists to do something so difficult as to be improbable?

*　*　*　*　*　*　*　*

174

Since the Renaissance, verse in English has most often used one of three methods of organization—by number of stresses, by number of syllables or by number and patterning of both. I aim to show that:

> I. Stress Verse usually corresponds closely to the rhythmic movement of the poem. Such verse is easily produced in English but its more common modes provide few of the tensions or excitements available in other forms. This, of course, does not preclude other sources of tension, excitement or personal characteristics.

> II. Syllabic Meter contributes very little to a poem's realized sound. Permitting any arhythmic movement, it also permits whatever rhythms the poet can produce but offers no help or encouragement in sustaining them.

> III. Syllabic-Stress Meter, the classical system of English prosody, offers fewer freedoms but has built-in opportunities both for establishing a rhythmic underlay and, because of its range of variations, for creating counter tensions and syncopations. This meter may yield a richer mix of music and meaning than many writers, raised in a culture whose music is based on highly simplified and regularized rhythms, might devise on their own. It can also tempt one into merely filling out a metrical paradigm and settling for the slack comforts of its regular patterns.

I will investigate the relation of each of these prosodies to the "music" and the meaning of particular poems, on occasion examining the work of major practitioners and considering how that form and music reflected their personal characteristics and needs.

I. Rhythms in Stress Verse

Stress, from earliest times, has been a salient feature of English as of most Germanic languages. Correspondingly, it has been a defining factor in our poetry, from the Anglo-Saxon Alliterative Meter down through such Middle English poems as *Piers Plowman* or *Sir Gawain and the Green Knight*. By the time of the Renaissance, however, learned and aristocratic writers had adopted Continental or classical prosodies based on number or duration of syllables. Stress Verse—also called Accentual or Qualitative Meter—persisted in the simpler folkish forms: nursery rhymes, folk songs and ballads, adages and cautionary verses. Those genres were later restored to literary fashion by the Romantic poets' reawakened interest in the folk arts and, in an extreme form, by Gerard Manley Hopkins' "Sprung Rhythm." They are still current in such forms as light verse, rap music and, alas, advertising jingles.

Stress is a natural and stable basis for English meter. Since it is directly related to meaning—linguists term it a distinctive factor— readers who understand a passage similarly will accent it in much the same way. Newcomers to the language or others who misplace stress—put the emPHAsis on the wrong sylLABle"—may be almost unintelligible. Beyond the inherent stresses, those marked by dictionaries, we enrich a statement's inferences, its subtexts, by the fine-tuning of stresses. We can sharply alter implications by extra stressing of any syllable: **SOME** girls were lovely (others were not); some **GIRLS** were lovely (women, men and boys were not); some girls **WERE** lovely (but no longer are); some girls were **LOVE**ly (in the extreme). Love**LEE** would suggest adolescent admiration approaching mockery.

Though all syllables in a statement convey meaning, stressed syllables usually carry information of a particular kind and order. The main nouns and verbs—those usually receiving the heaviest stress—convey information or opinion about the "outside" world or about the speaker's self. Thus the term "stress" not only applies to the way syllables are spoken but also to their significance and effect on hearers. This in turn affects our recording of memories: by means of certain "stress" hormones, events of higher emotional content are more deeply engraved in long-term memory. The added time usually given to stressed syllables—a matter which will concern us later—probably reflects both the natural length of "root" syllables from earlier quantitative languages, and also the added time needed to register such information. The coincidence of stress with meaning becomes clearer if we take an ordinary sentence— confined, for simplicity, to monosyllables—and emphasize its stressed syllables:

As I **came** to the **end** of the **road** I **saw** a **car hit** a **bus**.

By segregating these syllables

came . . . end . . . road . . . saw . . . car hit . . . bus

we devise a sort of telegraphese whose nouns and verbs report the objects and actions involved. Yet that could be misleading: we might wrongly suppose that the speaker (a) saw a car hit *by* a bus, (b) saw a car *and* hit a bus, (c) saw a car that got hit *and also* saw a bus, or, even, (d) saw *both* a car and a bus get hit. If polysyllabic words were involved, stresses would fall less predictably, yet stresses would still accrue most often to those crucial "root" syllables; stress and content would still generally coincide.

Unstressed syllables, such as articles, adjectives and adverbs, often supply modifications and less salient information about objects and actions. More significantly, however, participles, infinitives, conjunctions, etc., tell us how to build the "content" syllables into sentences. These lighter "function" syllables may seem less important, but they are indispensable in such matters as telling active from passive constructions—distinguishing who or what acted or was acted upon.

This difference between the information carried by stressed and unstressed syllables has its physical basis in the form and operation of areas of the brain developed at different periods of a baby's growth. Language is normally handled by networks of neuronal connections found throughout the brain but centering in Broca's and Wernicke's areas of the left hemisphere. Some (but only some) evidence suggests that unstressed syllables are controlled in Broca's area, which also handles sequencing in general and the production of speech sounds. Stressed syllables are more probably centered in Wernicke's area, which manages comprehension. For this discussion, the point lies not in locating the seat of these operations but in noting that these networks are discrete; through stroke or other physical injury, one can be lost while the other survives. The familiar PBS television series *The Brain* featured an interview with a patient who'd been accidentally injured in these areas. Obviously intelligent, he still grasped the informational content of the main nouns and verbs, but the loss of unstressed "function" syllables had disabled him for many routine activities, ending his career as a lawyer. It is significant that, in a given sentence, the words he could still record were precisely those we would mark with a stress if we were scanning it as a poem.

Distribution of stresses and nonstresses not only affects the knowledge imparted; since stress, as noted, usually brings duration with it, distribution also controls the quality of movement. The first half of the sentence analyzed above has fewer stresses, moving gracefully in a triple rhythm—in a poem, we might scan it as three anapests:

⌣ ⌣ / l ⌣ ⌣ / l ⌣ ⌣ / l
As I came to the end of the road

The second half is more tense because more compact with stress, culminating in the collision of stresses which report the vehicular impact:

⌣ / ⌣ / / ⌣ /
I saw a car hit a bus.

This is not to imply, as do some commentators, that speech rhythms, the "music" of verse, necessarily imitate and emphasize a poem's local dictionary sense. Examples are commonly taken from some of Alexander Pope's slighter imitative effects:

When Ajax strives some rock's vast weight to throw
The line too labors, and the words move slow
Not so, when swift Camilla scours the plain,
Flies o'er th' unbending corn, and skims along the main.

No one doubts the admirable virtuosity of Pope's lines. Yet the deeper business of music is not so much to emphasize meaning as to amplify it—not merely to underline the message content but often to extend and particularize it, making it more personal, less subject to assumption. We earlier noted how discretionary stresses can alter sense; that is reflected in the rhythm and may qualify, sometimes even reverse, overall meaning as it tempers the emotional tone.

Still, the coincidence of rhythm and meaning in the sentence about the auto accident is not fanciful; we might alter that sentence's movement:

I walked right down to the street's end and I saw that a car had demolished a bus. In the first half, such collected stress

ᵕ / / / ᵕ ᵕ / /
I walked right down to the street's end

seems misplaced unless there is some reason to emphasize that one did not pause along the way. The second half, with its balletic anapests

ᵕ / | ᵕ ᵕ / | ᵕ ᵕ / | ᵕ ᵕ / |
I saw that a car had demolished a bus

might suggest, if it appeared in a poem (where we become more responsive to such matters) an almost ghoulish delight in carnage. Indeed, a similar switch from a slower, heavier movement to a quick, light rhythm turns the last line of E. A. Robinson's "Richard Cory" into a delicious malice dance of envy and revenge:

So on we worked, and waited for the light,
And went without the meat, and cursed the bread;

And Richard Cory, one calm summer night,
   Went home and put a bullet through his head.

Even starker mismatches of rhythm and emotional tone contribute to the comic tone of William McGonagall's expressions of horror:

Oh, Heaven! it was a frightful and pitiful sight to see
Seven bodies charred of the Jarvis family;
And Mrs. Jarvis was found with her child, and both
   carbonized,
And as the searchers gazed thereon they were surprised.

We should turn, then, to the actual workings of Stress Verse. In such forms, the length and movement of lines are determined simply by the number of heavy stresses—lighter syllables falling between as they may. This brings into play several inbuilt habits of arranging stresses and nonstresses, so imparting definite rhythmic inclinations. In *Consciousness and the Computational Mind*, the linguist Ray Jackendoff notes that "stress is patterned: . . . languages tend to alternate stressed syllables with one or two unstressed syllables." In English, this might even, on extreme occasions, grow to as many as five or six. Further, English stresses *do* sometimes collide even though we sometime alter inherent stress to avoid this. (A standard example is "thirTEEN," which may change to "THIRteen MEN.") Despite exceptions, however, we do tend toward the ordering Jackendoff suggests—one or two light syllables between stresses. Such a numerical rhythm, tied to meaning, rises directly from the brain's habit of chunking items into sense groups. In poetry this numerical tendency often produces a movement rather like Gregorian chant or the "irregular" rhythms of certain non-Western musics.

Our language, however, also has an urge toward more regular musics—a principle called "time-stress" or "isochrony," which may compete, though in Stress Verse it more often cooperates, with the numerical patterning described above. This rhythm establishes stresses at roughly equal intervals, letting lighter syllables cram or stretch themselves between the main "beats." This is specially noticeable when voices become insistent or impassioned—when we "hammer home a point." If the number of weaker syllables varies widely from the usual one or two between stresses, the time between beats may well be affected. Nonetheless, this movement will tend to resemble the constant time-based rhythms of western popular or classical music.

This temporal habit has led some writers to theorize that poetry, by its nature, conforms to such regular rhythms. Indeed, Sidney Lanier offered musical notation for one of Shakespeare's sonnets. But that is to turn a propensity into a rigid theory, ignoring not only the looser numerical rhythms but also local speech variants and valid diversities of interpretation which may alter stress distribution and, thus, rhythm.

Isochronic theory reflects the fact that stress is produced not only by volume and pitch, but also, as already noted, by duration. On average, our stressed syllables are twice as long as the unstressed. That is true, however, only on the average—actual lengths differ widely and may be changed by the pressures of usage, of surrounding syllables, and varying interpretations. Indeed, in some cases, a particular stressed syllable may actually be shorter than a specific unstressed one, as in the word "pittance." Yet the normal coincidence of length with stress did lead certain Renaissance poets (besides a few recent ones) to attempt poems in Greek or Latin forms. Only a few of Thomas Campion's "aires" employ this prosody successfully—clearly because they scan almost identically whether by stress or by length.

The British scholar Derek Attridge has produced two studies which, despite a quirky and complicated method of scansion, offer strong insights. Not least is his recognition of the link between Stress Verse and the common 4 x 4 stanza: four lines, each with four stress units or substituted pauses. This stanza, found in many folk songs, hymns or poems based on those forms, is usually built from a half-line unit of two stresses, which is then doubled and redoubled into larger segments. The ballad "Little Mattie Groves" offers a standard model:

O holy day, high holiday,
    The best day of the year,

> Little Mattie Groves to church did go
> Some holy words to hear.

After the first line's caesura, the two-stress unit is repeated, giving a full line of four stresses. The second line has no caesura, but the fourth stress is replaced by a pause. This two-line segment is then replicated for lines three and four.

The first stanza of the ballad "The Unquiet Grave" generally conforms:

> Cold are the winds of night, true love;
> Cold are the drops of rain;
> The very first love that ever I had,
> In greenwood he lies slain.

Here, at variance with Attridge's description, the caesura and the break into half-lines (derived from Anglo-Saxon alliterative meter) are missing. As before, lines 2 and 4 have no caesura but end in a pause. Further variants are possible: lines 2 and 4 sometimes have a fourth stress; lines 1, 2 and 4 may all have three stresses and a pause while only line 3 has all four stresses.

In any case, these groups (half-line, line, two-line and four-line segments) habitually coincide with units of syntax and of rhythm. Since these derive from the rhythms inherent to the language and, moreover, frequently rise from a numerical rhythm to a temporal isochrony, Stress Verse is a natural choice for song; indeed, such forms as folk ballads and nursery rhymes were originally sung. The best known version of "The Unquiet Grave" has this melody:

Though other measures are common—ballad singers often have their own versions of text and / or music—the music here slips easily into triple rhythms. Rests or longer notes at the ends of lines 2 and 4 fill out the musical cadence as they do the textual meter, giving a steady pattern of 4 x 4 musical bars as of verse lines. Shorter passing notes may be added or several notes tied into a ligature to adjust the melody to changes in syllable count or to secondary stresses ("true love" or "very first love"). Stress variations (especially if the music is in faster tempi) are, however, usually kept to a minimum by the needs and habits of singers in English.

It might seem—and sometimes *is*—an advantage that poetic meter, speech rhythm and musical measure all fit together so readily. While both rhythmic tendencies already noted (numerical and rhythmical) take effect and cooperate, a pleasant, sustaining rhythm is offered, ready-made and pretty much guaranteed throughout. That is precisely the problem: it *is* easy and ready-made—little that's exciting, subtle, or personally characteristic is to hand.

An old adage says, "The more music, the less meaning." This has a measure—though *only* a measure—of truth; the interaction between music and meaning is not easily summed up. We have seen that altered stresses (thus, altered rhythms) can provide depth of connotation, of emotion and character underlying the literal and conscious. Qualities of voice such as rhythm and movement often indicate, willy-nilly, a speaker's authenticity. We might recall the use of melody in teaching a language, in preventing stuttering, or in recovering speech and memory after a stroke or other physical injury. Indeed, there are reasons to say, "The more music, the more meaning," though this raises the question of *kinds* of meaning, of what we mean by "meaning."

In any case, a rhythm which becomes unobstructed and habitual, or which is overemphasized, loses immediacy and, with it, meaning and its retention. It is as if the brain recognizes in subtle or varied rhythms, particularly those involving complication of stresses, its own methods; in a mechanical or rigidly expectable rhythm it senses something alien, an abstract or willful order, and so lets it pass by, not leaving much trace. As a prank, the English poet George MacBeth sometimes read his poems (clearly iambic) as if all syllables were the same length. The result was so disorienting that little was retained beyond a sense of estrangement. In other poets' present-day readings something similar, though unintended, often happens with another aspect of stress—pitch. Some readers, feeling that poetry should be more musical than prose, impose an artificially repeated pattern of pitches; within three sentences, all recognition or retention of meaning evaporates.

The easy repetition of simple rhythmic patterns in Stress Verse may partially justify the classical metrists' prejudice against it—though that is also driven by a snobbish bias against the folk arts and a hankering for prestigious terminology. More significantly, however, the freedoms which Stress Verse offer—you can always throw in a few extra light syllables—provide only a narrow range of meaningful variation. It lets a poet do the natural and easy thing—so excusing him or her from the unnatural, peculiar, intensely personal thing.

Such modes arise from and continue to reflect a "folk community"—an earlier, less varied society with less demand for (and so less restraint against) extremes of personality, less conflict between the manner, language and musics of parent and child. Folk ballads and songs often included the communal voice of a chorus; in English, delivery was undramatic and impersonal, diverting little attention from the story and its message to the singer's style or vocal qualities. Other aspects of such songs may display great individual brilliancies: the powerful structure of "Edward" or "Lord Randall," the brilliant imagery of "Sir Patrick Spens," the sudden revelatory details of "Little Mattie Groves" or "Frankie and Johnnie." The ballads' rhythms, however, seldom yield comparable excellences; they reflect the steadier, less exploratory ways of a life more confined by economic necessity.

As noted earlier, Stress Verse was restored to literary fashion by the early Romantic poets; their usage, though fairly conservative, still provided a relief from the rigidities of Neo-classicism. Yet by the latter part of the nineteenth century, that easy movement and undistinguished grace were proving almost equally inimical to personal expression—almost definitive of the Romantic impulse in the arts. Poets began to experiment with variants which might bring different aspects of the verse (e.g., the numerical and the musical) into conflict.

Alfred, Lord Tennyson, in a verse which obviously influenced Whitman and helped spark further experiment, laid down three heavy monosyllablic stresses to establish an isochronic rhythm which carries through the poem:

BREAK, BREAK, BREAK

Break, break, break,
On thy cold gray stones, O Sea!
And I would that my tongue could utter
The thoughts that arise in me.

O well for the fisherman's boy,
That he shouts with his sister at play!
O well for the sailor lad,
That he sings in his boat on the bay!

And the stately ships go on
To their haven under the hill;
But O for the touch of a vanished hand,
And the sound of a voice that is still!

Break, break, break,
At the foot of thy crags, O Sea!
But the tender grace of a day that is dead
Will never come back to me.

This proves, finally, to be another variant of the 4 x 4 stanza, though here most lines replace the fourth stress with a full break and pause. Although the main beats remain quite constant, more and more light syllables are sifted in between: lines grow from three syllables all the way to eleven. As we approach the climactic lines, each with four full stresses,

> But O for the touch of a vanished hand,

and

> But the tender grace of a day that is dead

so many light syllables have interposed that, out of context, we'd call these lines anapestic. And though they do have some of the "bounce" usually so troublesome in triple meters, Tennyson cannily turns that to express not the usual high spirits but, rather, the speaker's envious anger against anyone spared his grief.

Those numerical differences are essential; other variants are found only in the secondary stresses at the poem's beginning and end, so providing an envelope of heavier gesture. The characterizing effect is clearly heard if some of those lighter, swifter syllables are removed, substituting what seems an iambic movement:

> Break, break, break,
>   On cold, gray stones, O sea!
> I would my tongue could speak
>   The thoughts that rise in me.
>
> It's well the fisher's boy
>   Can shout with friends at play;
> It's well the sailor lad
>   Can sing across the bay
>
> While stately ships sail on
>   To port beneath the hill
> But O to touch a vanished hand
>   And hear a voice that's still.
>
> Break, break, break,
>   Below thy crags, O Sea!
> The tender grace of days long dead
>   Will not come back to me.

Without that surging rhythm, Tennyson's rush of bitter emotion completely vanishes.

In a poem from *The Heart of Midlothian*, Sir Walter Scott contrives a variety of Stress Verse less emphatically stressed than Tennyson's walloping isochronics. This technique owes much to rougher, less "regular" examples of folk balladry ("Proud Maisrie" does appear as a character in the folk ballad, "The Gairdener Childe").

PROUD MAISRIE

Proud Maisrie is in the wood,
    Walking so early;
Sweet Robin sits on the bush,
    Singing so rarely.

"Tell me, thou bonny bird,
    When shall I marry me?"
"When six braw gentlemen
    Kirkward shall carry ye."

"Who makes the bridal bed,
    Birdie, say truly?"
"The gray-headed sexton
    That delves the grave duly.

"The glowworm o'er grave and stone
    Shall light thee steady;
The owl from the steeple sing
    'Welcome, proud lady.'"

This offers a tighter stanza than those already considered: lines 1 and 3 have three stresses; 2 and 4 only two. The disposition of strong and weak syllables is more varied and subtle; the rhythmic tendencies noted earlier (numerical and isochronic) are suggested, but never fully established. The very first line presents a problem:

we hear three stresses, but two of them collide immediately, "Proud Mais-"; that is followed, moreover, by four nonstresses. In the parallel line 3, "Sweet" must be counted a secondary stress; should we then treat "Proud" similarly? Or can we claim that "in" may be a trifle stronger than the words around it ("is" and "the") and so should count as a conventional stress? Might we suggest that heavy beats throughout the poem are allowed to shift to a syllable earlier or later than expected? Could we say that the second full beat falls into a pause after the girl's name?

I suggest that we slough off such rationalizations, none of which helps us understand or describe what happens in the verse. No poet's mission lies in supplying material from which critics and students can demonstrate capability or extract rules. Ambiguity of movement is precisely what gives Scott's verse its natural and variable charm. Undeniably, the latent stress pattern continues in one's expectations throughout the poem. This, then, requires the speaker's sense of rhythm and gesture to preserve the gist of a music which hovers above – both affirming and evading—the underlying pattern. (And which resembles, incidentally, some of the syncopations we will hear in the Syllabic-Stress meters.) This latent stress gives a speaker (or a song composer) an additional problem—i.e., an opportunity. For Tennyson's poem we could readily provide musical notation applicable to all stanzas and corresponding to what most readers hear. Scott's supple rhythms and alliterations offer a hesitant and echoing charm that would be harder to notate or to set—neither absent nor insistent, a tactful but inescapable influence.

No doubt the most provocative elaboration of Stress Verse is found in the Sprung Rhythm of Hopkins. Into this usually unobtrusive form Hopkins imported many effects from our classical Syllabic-Stress prosody or from free verse, so creating some of our most idiosyncratic poems. Hearing an unfamiliar verse of Hopkins', we might guess its author as confidently as we do the work of Bach, Brahms or Fauré.

We should consider, first, some of Hopkins' more conventional Stress Verse.

INVERSNAID

This darksome burn, horseback brown,
His rollrock highroad roaring down,
In coop and in comb the fleece of his foam
Flutes and low to the lake falls home.

A windpuff-bonnet of fáwn-fróth
Turns and twindles over the broth
Of a pool so pitchblack, féll-frówning,
It rounds and rounds Despair to drowning.

Degged with dew, dappled with dew
Are the groins of the braes that the brook treads through,
Wiry heathpacks, flitches of fern,
And the beadbonny ash that sits over the burn.

What would the world be, once bereft
Of wet and of wildness: Let them be left,
O let them be left, wildness and wet;
Long live the weeds and the wilderness yet.

The poem's eccentricity of sentiment, vocabulary and syntax would readily identify its author; its movement might not—we might mistake this for any of several late nineteenth century poets. This is another version of the 4 x 4 stanza: four heavy accents per line, one to three syllables per foot or stress unit. Again, one could easily offer musical notation representing the movement most readers hear. Measures of equal lengths would show either duple ("heathpacks") or triple ("flitches of") rhythms; secondary stresses—"burn, horseback brown" or "rollrock highroad roaring"—would yield light syncopations. The tensions produced, common enough in English to draw little conscious attention, yield a delightful, surging energy.

Hopkins' more arbitrary techniques are suggested, however, by his marking of stresses:

A windpuff-bonnet of fáwn-fróth

and

> Of a pool so pitchblack, féll-frówning,

Most readers, I suspect, simply ignore such markings, yet wider questions are involved. In his preface, Hopkins posits that the four major stresses per line are to be isochronic—positioned equally in time:

> In Sprung Rhythm, as in logaoedic rhythm [i.e., Stress Verse] generally, the feet are assumed to be equally long or strong and their seeming inequality is made up by pause or stressing.

In marking such stresses, Hopkins intends the two final stresses ("fáwn-fróth") to occupy as much time as the first two feet ("A wind-puff bonnet of") while, again, "féll-frówning" must equal "Of a pool so pitchblack." In actual reading, such durations would feel labored and artificial. If he had wished, Hopkins could easily have given these final half-lines equal length by adding syllables: " fawn-colored froth," "fawnlike frothiness" or "so furiously frowning." Yet this, too, would have been clumsy. Even though the stress collisions he chose instead clearly create the variations his ear desired, he still felt a need to account for their irregularity.

Even in poems specified as Sprung Rhythm Hopkins clearly felt a need for such markings:

> Márgarét, áre you griéving

Many readers would give this line only two accents, though a third (with a slight change of emphasis) might fall on "are." Hopkins' line, on its own, has an emotional and tender grace which would be lost with four actual stresses

> Dearest Marg'ret, why be grieving
> Over Goldengrove unleaving . . .

Hopkins' enforced stresses, meant to sanction a forbidden excellence, are rather like Milton's theoretical contractions or elisions, permitting greater freedom of movement—though Milton had the example, at least, of Puritan psalms and of Italian versification, where such sounds are actually contracted.

In other poems which Hopkins designated as Sprung Rhythm, especially those with lines of five and six stresses, the spoken rhythms become even more eccentric and their rationalization more controversial. Projecting extremes of personal ecstasy or despair, Hopkins quite abandons the untroubled flow of most Stress Verse. Not only does he bring stresses into jarring collisions—even ten-syllable smash-ups—but he allows stress units to take on extra syllables and stresses (designated as "hangers" and "outrides"), so forming loops of graceful or less defined movement. His stresses, thus "sprung" from regular recurrence, take on far greater salience and emotional intensity. This, at least in part, Hopkins learned from work in Syllabic-Stress Verse where he found such bunchings and relaxations essential in avoiding the "same and tame."

The rhythm of his poems is also less than usually controlled by line endings. Rhymes—often extravagant, sometimes downright desperate—may suggest line breaks; this, however, is countered by lines which are (either by Hopkins' fiat or his syntax) enjambed or "rove over"; meantime, internal or nonce rhymes are often as prominent as end-rhymes. Similar oppositions appear in the use of larger forms: we find sonnets in alexandrines, sonnets in Sprung Rhythm, sonnets with two codas, curtal sonnets of ten and a half lines, etc.

But we should turn to an example of Hopkins more eccentric practice:

THE WINDHOVER

I caught this morning morning's minion, king-
   dom of daylight's dauphin, dapple-dawn-drawn
     Falcon, in his riding
   Of the rolling level underneath him steady air, and
     striding

High there, how he rung upon the rein of a wimpling
    wing
In his ecstacy! then off, off forth on swing,
    As a skate's heel sweeps smooth on a bow-bend: the
      hurl and gliding
    Rebuffed the big wind. My heart in hiding
Stirred for a bird,—the achieve of, the mastery of the
    thing.

Brute beauty and valour and act, oh, air, pride, plume,
    here
    Buckle! AND the fire that breaks from thee then, a billion
Times told lovelier, more dangerous, O my chevalier!
    No wonder of it: shéer plód makes plough down sillion
Shine, and blue-bleak embers, ah my dear,
    Fall, gall themselves and gash gold-vermilion.

Hopkins opens this poem of daring meters and rhythms, as
Whitman often did, with a reassuring line of what seems iambic
pentameter:

I caught this morning morning's minion, king-

The following lines, however, immediately reject any such familiar
form; Hopkins' notes on the poem as "Falling Paeonic rhythm,
sprung and outriding" offer little help. If prosody can be so com-
pletely divorced from the actual sound, what line in English could
not be labeled "Paeonic"? True, certain feet in the poem can be taken
for First, or Falling Paeons (/ ⌣ ⌣ ⌣): "dauphin, dapple" "Falcon in
his" or "rung upon the." Yet such feet were already validated by the
term "Sprung Rhythm," indicating that stress units may vary from
one to four syllables. Most questionable is Hopkins' self-contradic-
tory designation of "AND" in line 10 as "a non-metrical stress"; this
word, capitalized as the strongest stress in the poem, is not to be
counted at all.
    We've already mentioned the old adage that "the more music,
the less meaning"; admittedly, paeonic meters (or anapests and

dactyls, for that matter) can easily become mechanical, almost nonsensical. Poe's "The Bells" is the standard example, or we could again summon the ghost of McGonagall for a comically juxtaposed paeonic line:

> On the last Sabbath day of 1879,
> Which will be remembered for a very long time.

As more syllables are squeezed between stresses, all syllables are unnaturally shortened. If many paeons follow one another the produced rhythm tends toward $\frac{2}{4}$♪♪♪♪|♪♪♪♪| and all syllables, strong or weak, tend to become equal in length; stressed syllables, deprived of normal duration, are less prominent and may lack the time for their semantic freight to be fully recorded. Hopkins, admitting only occasional paeons and using various ways to impede their rush, gains flexibility but again conjures up metrical peculiarities he must explain away.

Fortunately, we need not justify the ways of the poet to his or her readers. D. W. Harding writes in *Words Into Rhythm*:

> [Hopkins] worked out . . . [an] elaborate prosodic defense of a practise that must have come about spontaneously through his magnificent control of the rhythms of the language. . . . How his nominal prosody helps in the reading of his verse or why his verse should need formal prosodic justification it is not nowadays easy to see.

We are concerned, primarily, with the poem's created rhythm, and only secondarily with whatever rationalizations made those sounds permissible. Common sense urges that we see the poem simply as having five main stresses per line but with extraordinary variations between them.

Our attention must lie with rhythmic currents which may bear little relation to repetitions of feet, to stress units, or to whatever movement one might suppose inheres to lines. After the commonplace sound pattern of the poem's opening, "I caught this morning," we should be aware how this is developed into a brilliant succession of variants:

⌣　⌣　/　⌣　　/　⌣
-dom of daylight's dauphin,

/　⌣　/　　/　　/　⌣
dapple-dawn-drawn falcon

⌣　⌣　/　⌣
in his riding

⌣　⌣　/　⌣　/　⌣
of the rolling, level

/　⌣　/　⌣　/　⌣　/
underneath him steady air

⌣　　/　⌣
and striding

This is what the reader hears and should attend. In a line like:

Times told lovelier, more dangerous, O my chevalier!

our proper concern is with how the heavy initial stresses ("Times told love-") burst into excited loops of light syllables—"lovelier, more dangerous"—then into the breathless "O my chevalier!"

It is ironic, but typical of Hopkins, that he should adopt the usually impersonal Stress Verse and, then, through the projection of his own emotional, self-assertive and contrary nature, transform that prosody into a medium for the most highly conflicted and anomalous verses. Robert Bridges, who preserved and eventually brought Hopkins' work to publication, spoke of the poems' "naked encounter of sensualism and ascetiscism"—also intimating much of Hopkins' style in matters religious or philosophic. Early, he abandoned his family's deep Anglican ties to become a Jesuit; soon, however, he took as his spiritual authority John Duns Scotus, a figure previously considered heretical and still spurned. Maintaining his position in a church which located divinity in universal qualities, Hopkins himself affirmed and celebrated divinity in the individual and eccentric. The position suggests its own reductio ad absurdum: we are all alike in being so different, all united in a common separation.

Hopkins, then, invented exciting musics not heard elsewhere despite (or, characteristically, by means of) committing himself to a metrical system. Like many others (e.g., Marianne Moore, whom we will shortly consider) his deep need for restraints and formal structures was probably involved with sexual questions. Unlike Moore, however, Hopkins' drive against those very restraints remained powerful; he showed every sign of sustaining, while containing, a strongly sensual (frequently homosexual) presence. Often, he seems to have employed such contradictions to restrain himself in one area only to free himself in another.

By his elaborate terminology, Hopkins intended to prove—like Milton before him—that his licenses were really conformities to rules he could claim to have uncovered. Like his model, Hopkins built and rigidly observed elaborate imaginary fences so that he could leap those laid out by others. Or devised new systems of bookkeeping for public inspection while carrying on daily operations to the business's best profit and advantage.

Some may regret that Hopkins expended so much energy conceiving fictions which let him write what he wished. Very few, indeed, are in a position to suggest how Hopkins could have written better poems. Isaiah Berlin has drawn attention to the way that the mind is always caught between competing value systems; one would suspect that the more capacious or powerful the mind, the fiercer might be that competition. It is to be expected, moreover, that in a poet's work, this struggle may appear most strikingly in less conscious areas such as rhythmical and musical practices. Even if we do not accept the fictions which gave Hopkins the desired permissions, they helped produce the most memorable rhetoric and vocal music in English since the time of Christopher Smart—another religious zealot who mastered several forms of prosody in which to depict the birds and animals as figuring forth holy powers. To have equaled Smart's sonority and exaltation, without the support of a previously established meter or of close-rhyming stanzas, is well worth whatever contrivances it required or the despairs it entailed.

II. RHYTHMS IN SYLLABIC METER

In English, Syllabic Verse is a twentieth-century import and something of an oddity. Derived chiefly from the French, where word stress is minimal, it ignores accent or stress, counting only the number of syllables in each line or half line. The prosody, then, tells almost nothing about a poem's created rhythm. In many such poems, every line will have the same number of syllables; examples are readily found in W. H. Auden, Donald Justice, Thom Gunn, Kenneth Rexroth, Dylan Thomas, and George P. Elliott, though in longer poems some allow an occasional syllable more or less. However, a syllabic poem may build stanzas whose lines have differing lengths; in succeeding stanzas, corresponding lines will have the same count. For instance, in "To a Steamroller," Marianne Moore used four-line stanzas, unrhymed, with five, twelve, twelve and fifteen syllables per line. In "The Fish," a rhymed poem, she used five-line stanzas of one, three, nine, six and eight syllables. Though syllabic forms had earlier been used by Robert Bridges, his daughter Elizabeth Daryush, and by Edith Sitwell, Moore introduced these forms to the United States and used them most extensively and daringly; I will take my examples from her work.

As we've noted, stress in English reflects semantic weight and emphasis. Since, in our speech, this is produced by a combination of loudness, length and pitch, it controls not only the current of meaning but also the flow of rhythmic movement. When stresses fall at random, one can create, or may equally forgo, rhythmic patterns and corresponding musical intensities; in most cases, the reader is not led to expect regularity or recurrence. If, when reading aloud, one were to pause after each line, listeners might at least be aware of (and so have expectations about) line lengths. However, such formal pauses are actively discouraged by typography: lines don't usually start with capitals nor do their endings coincide with syntactic groupings.

It is almost as if the poet wrote free verse while satisfying some requirement unrelated to the poem's sound—say, how many letters and spaces per line, how many words per stanza, or how often a verb or noun, even some particular letter, could appear in a line or stanza. Donald Hall has written poems which fix the number of syllables not for single lines but for pairs of lines; Robert Francis sometimes fixed the number of words (not syllables) per line. Grace Schulman's study, *Marianne Moore: The Poetry of Engagement*, shows that Moore, in revision, sometimes dropped the syllabic shaping altogether, instead printing a particular poem or passage as free verse in which line breaks *do* coincide with syntax. In a poem about her cat, "Peter," the original syllabic version of one passage runs:

> Profound sleep is
> not with him, a fixed illusion. Springing about with
> froglike ac-
>
> curacy, emitting jerky cries when taken in the hand, he is
> himself
> again; to sit caged by the rungs of a domestic chair would
> be unprofit-
> able—human. What is the good of hypocrisy? It
> is permissible to choose one's employment, to abandon
> the wire nail, the
> roly-poly, when it shows signs of being no longer
> a pleas-
>
> ure, to score the adjacent magazine with a double line of strokes.

Revised, so that line endings do coincide with breaks in the sense, this becomes:

Profound sleep is not with him a fixed illusion.
Springing about with froglike accuracy, with jerky cries
when taken in hand, he is himself again;
to sit caged by the rungs of a domestic chair
would be unprofitable—human. What is the good of
    hypocrisy?
It is permissible to choose one's employment,
to abandon the wire nail, the roly-poly,
when it shows signs of being no longer a pleasure,
to score the adjacent magazine with a double line of strokes.

The reordered lines, though more easily understood, lose much of the eccentric and spiky character of both cat and poet.

We should, perhaps, have expected the personal to reside in such less conscious areas of technique. Critics have often remarked on how much William Carlos Williams' verse gains from similar conflicts of syntax and line shaping. Linguists have noted the personalizing effect of concurrence and conflict (termed "interference") between such elements as the metrical and syntactic, aesthetic and cognitive. Further, the effort of "decoding" such lines often enhances our realization of their personal meaning. John D. Barrows, in *The Artful Universe*, noting that listening to music often improves performance in unrelated areas, writes, "The brain has clearly developed an extraordinary facility for sequential and parallel timing of different movements, combining them to produce a single continuous activity like that required to serve a tennis ball." Or to serve or receive the conflicted texture and content of a poem.

Poems in Syllabic Meter may, of course, embody any stricter form. In "A Carriage from Sweden," Marianne Moore writes what are, to all intents, jingling iambic tetrameters:

They say there is a sweeter air
    where it was made, than we have here;
a Hamlet's castle atmosphere.

or again in "Spencer's Ireland":

the kindest place I've never been,
the greenest place I've never seen.

Syllabic poems, however, are equally free to maintain a proselike movement while fulfilling elaborate stanza patterns, as in the beginning of this poem whose title is part of the first sentence:

THE MONKEYS

winked too much and were afraid of snakes. The zebras,
    supreme in
their abnormality; the elephants in their fog-colored skin

Each of the poem's four 6-line stanzas begins with a 10-syllable line; each second line has 11 syllables and rhymes with the first, though this may be, as here, disguised. This liberty to be as musical or as prosy as one desires results directly from the fact that stresses fall at random, regardless of their disposition in other lines or stanzas. "Spencer's Ireland," for instance, has six complex 12-line stanzas, the sixth line of each stanza broken by a visible caesura into rhyming half-lines: three syllables before, four syllables after. If we extract the sixth line from each stanza:

the culprit;   nor blows, but it
there be fern   seed for unlearn-
perfection,   one objection
of the fly   for mid-July
lunulae   aren't jewelry
them invis-   ible; they've dis-

we find no correspondence between their syntax or their rhythmic movement: as elsewhere in the poem, rhymes may be either conspicuous or barely noticeable; several of the internal rhymes will be recognized only by a diligent eye. The line from stanza 1, quoted above, is part of the sentence: "Denunciations do not affect / *the culprit; nor blows, but it* / is torture to him not to be spoken to." (Italics mine.) Even more drastically, the line from stanza 6 comes from the sentence: "Discommodity makes / *them invis-ible; they've dis- /* appeared." We have a slant rhyme, buried in weak syllables and disguised by hyphenation across the caesura.

In some instances, the rhymes, even though they fall on un-stressed syllables, may take on a special tang as the syntax and phrasing flow over, through and around the fixed grid of syllables. One such example begins:

THE FISH

wade
through black jade.
  Of the crow-blue mussel-shells, one keeps
  adjusting the ash-heaps;
      opening and shutting itself like

an
injured fan.
  The barnacles which encrust the side
  of the wave, cannot hide
      there for the submerged shafts of the

sun,
split like spun
  glass, move themselves with spotlight swiftness
  into the crevices —
      in and out, illuminating

the
turquoise sea
  of bodies. The water drives a wedge
  of iron through the iron edge
      of the cliff; whereupon the stars,

> pink
> rice-grains, ink
>   bespattered jelly-fish, crabs like green
>   lilies, and submarine
>   toadstools, slide each on the other.

And so on through three more stanzas. At first, rhymes fall conventionally, on stresses at line breaks coinciding with syntactic pauses, as in more traditional meters:

> The fish wade
> Through black jade.

The second stanza, however, lets rhymes fall on unstressed syllables; in the third, divergence of line and syntax gives the rhymes surprising piquancy. By the fifth stanza, the runovers make end-rhymes sound like initial rhymes:

> pink rice-grains,
> ink-bespattered jelly-fish . . .

These freedoms permit some of Moore's most exciting passages. In "His Shield," the opening rhythm, which practically begs to be sung, heralds a joyous parade of armored animals.

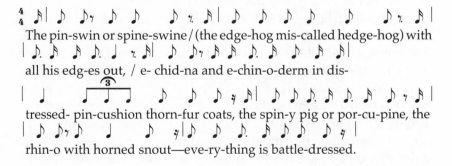

The pin-swin or spine-swine / (the edge-hog mis-called hedge-hog) with
all his edg-es out, / e- chid-na and e-chin-o-derm in dis-
tressed- pin-cushion thorn-fur coats, the spin-y pig or por-cu-pine, the
rhin-o with horned snout—eve-ry-thing is battle-dressed.

Though the announced rhythm, "The pin-swin or pine-swine . . ." may echo that of the opening of "The Fish," these long musical phrases are not much like anything else in our poetry. We do, however, often find similar rhythms in our music. Such phrases might derive from a children's rhyme or a popular song like "A-tisket, a-tasket, I lost my yellow basket"; for that matter, the pattern turns up in Beethoven's First Piano Concerto and many other classical sources.

Even more musically daring—like a drum riff from a marching band or bugle corps—is this passage declaring that there is "No Swan So Fine":

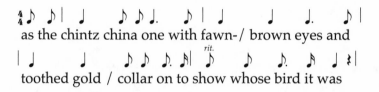

as the chintz china one with fawn- / brown eyes and

toothed gold / collar on to show whose bird it was

I would not readily give up such caperings or similar passages from "The Mind Is an Enchanting Thing" or "A Carriage from Sweden." Yet such musics are difficult to sustain or to reconcile with other rhythms and tones of voice, especially in a poem of serious moral intention. Poets who've followed Moore in syllabics have usually surrendered (or proven incapable of) such lively musics, producing poems more unified in tone and sound texture. In narratives and longer poems one doesn't ask for such local brilliancies; in shorter and lyrical poems, their lack is felt.

Yet even in her shorter poems, I often have trouble getting such passages to gear with the ideas expressed or with her more typically dry, a-musical style—even though that style connotes, at times, a comic inflation and pretension. On one hand, I hear the childlike song-and-dance rollcall of battle-dressed animals; on the other, a self-consciously Latinate diction, a detached, moralistic tone and arhythmic movement instructing me in the proper opinions—e.g., not to be armed with a measuring rod. Such morals seem to have little relevance to the world outside the poem, where the specific animals (humans among them) must struggle for their own and their kind's physical survival. This contrast of styles, together with certain habits of imagery, seems part of a general withdrawal from physicality or from animals as animals (rather than as emblems of moral qualities) which troubled even such admirers as Randall Jarrell.

Meantime, I sense no continuum of sound to underlie and sustain the different kinds of impulse; the contrast between these manners, failing to erect a universe of sound, remains a gap. This is caused, in large part, by Moore's rejection of the stress patterns which might have built a basic foundation of movement to contain or bridge these stylistic extremes. Of course, the iambic couplets quoted earlier do display stress patterns; yet those *are* exceptions. Couplets equally "correct" might have been written by any beginning student of English; in Moore's poems they seem like a regional spice sprinkled into a foreign recipe.

In the recordings Moore made of her poems, her lack of stress in speech actually makes it hard to understand her. Donald Hall—and there is corroboration from William Empson and Elizabeth Bishop—suggests that this may point to an incapacity to recognize speech stress. That might also explain her puzzling claim that she never did and never would write Syllabic Verse. Hall goes on to assert that Moore "made great art not only out of high ambitions, strong ideas and hard work but out of involuntary alienation." The title of his essay, "Marianne Moore Valiant and Alien," seems a necessary supplement to Schulman's "poetry of engagement." No doubt Moore *aimed* at engagement; her withdrawal from the physical, her insistence on "correctness," yields a sense of detachment, almost of removal.

The puzzle remains: in her student verses, Moore clearly *did* recognize and regularly used stress. That makes her disavowal of Syllabic Verse even more jarring; though she made other dubitable comments about her poems, none are so easily disproven. Perhaps, as she grew older and her mother's strictures against the physical intensified her own demands for self-abnegation, the use of stress in her speech—even her awareness of such qualities in others—may have diminished. That may well be a part of what Hall means by "involuntary alienation."

Moore's situation surprisingly resembled that of Whitman's (whom she called a literary grandfather) and, though her response obviously differed from his, must also have involved attitudes to sex and physicality. Like Whitman, Moore lived in New York City with her mother during that parent's lifetime, deriving knowledge of the world at large from zoos, museums, lectures and learned books. In his poems, Whitman—a vigorous physical presence who could not or would not restrict his sexual feelings, his daily patterns of working, eating or attendance into conventional patterns— refused any consistent patterning of either stress or syllable count. As with Whitman, Moore's early poems clearly recognized stress, though she, too, was unable to arrange them into patterns reflecting her own qualities. Apparently epicene and conventionally respectable, she chose to forgo stress patterns, but imposed elaborate restrictions of syllable count upon herself.

In both Whitman's and Moore's cases, the mother's role and embodiment in the produced work seem crucial. To enlist his mother in his poems, Whitman concocted a person quite unlike the woman in whose Brooklyn house he lived—one who could not have approved his ideas, poems, or affectional life. In contrast, Moore fully recognized her mother and adopted her principles— not only expressing those values in her work, but even allowing her to supply lines in the poems. Though she cites the opinions of her father, she never met the man. She did not always accede to her mother's dicta: Charles Molesworth, in *Marianne Moore: A Literary Life*, notes that all her life she sought areas where she dared develop some elements of separation. But woe be unto others who did not submit to that authority. When asked why a longtime friend had been excluded from their apartment, she replied indignantly, "Why, he disagreed with mother!"

Having gone so far, I will hazard a further speculation. John D. Barrows, whom I quoted earlier, remarking that every known society has had well-developed musical and rhythmic practices, skills with little apparent value for survival yet with surprising advantages, writes:

> [T]here is undeniably some prenatal conditioning of
> the human fœtus to the body rhythms of the mother,
> because they are regular enough to be recognized in

the presence of other irregular noises. Moreover these body rhythms restrict our music in definite ways. The division of melodies into musical phrases tends to produce intervals of time that are similar to the human breathing cycle. . . .

The child psychologist Lee Salk writes of those musics found in societies throughout the world:

[F]rom the most primitive tribal drumbeats to the symphonies of Mozart and Beethoven there is a startling similarity to the rhythm of the human heart. . . . [T]he maternal heartbeat, with respect to the fetal nervous system, occupies a place of primacy and constancy and may be associated with a feeling of well-being.

From the moment of birth, a baby recognizes its mother's voice; any prolonged separation of the two may interrupt the child's normal development. Later, most babies want to be carried where they can hear the mother's heartbeat, meanwhile developing responses to other rhythmic and musical sources. From their "dance of communication"—of reactive gestures and sounds—the child's language is developed, first with the mother, then with the world in general.

Writing about Whitman's "Out of the Cradle Endlessly Rocking," I have suggested that for poets—perhaps for humans in general—the urge to create such rhythms involves a re-creation (a mockingbird's song?) of that maternal body rhythm and of that sound's ambience. Thus, for the moment, we may be contained within and encompassed by what we take for a universal rhythm. I cannot quell a suspicion that Miss Moore stayed so close physically and metaphysically to that sound's original, had so firmly ingested that ambience, that she may have felt little need for surrogates, for substitutes from the physical world outside.

Unquestionably, Moore felt a need for restraints—felt that she, like the Hercules of her poem, must be "hindered to succeed." Syllabic patterning provided just the set of hurdles which often invigorated her lines. Many believe that getting rid of such hindrances will make an artist more creative. If art is to imitate life, that is at best doubtful; how better do we know others than by their coping with hindrances? Yet this, too, is an individual matter; some have benefitted while others wilted, under "the gentle tyranny" of rhyme—or of Syllabic-Stress Meter. If that "tyranny" conferred no other blessings, it often prevented us from accepting our first thoughts—for many, thoughts which others told us we should think.

It is surely to Marianne Moore's credit that she found a system which ignored the stress-patterns for which she seems not especially gifted. Though, like most freedoms, this brought its own problems, it allowed her often to use her eccentric gifts for striking rhythmic effects not possible under a more defining system—and not heard from any other poet.

III. RHYTHMS IN SYLLABIC-STRESS METER

As its name declares, Syllabic-Stress Meter controls both the number and the patterning of syllables and stresses in a line. Our inherent tendency to separate strong syllables by inserting light syllables between them is here more strictly alternated: in iambs and trochees, one weaker syllable falls between stresses; in anapests and dactyls, two fall there. As in Stress Verse, this patterning suggests a latent rhythmical basis throughout the poem. Yet, as Gerard Manley Hopkins noted, such strict organization may well grow "same and tame." Paradoxically, the system's rigidity has led to a wide range of exceptions and substitutions to diversify and liven the underlying rhythmic pulse. The resulting sprints and hurdles, bursts and pauses, offer a broad spectrum of personal, dramatic, discursive and meditative qualities. Rules that may have been intended to restrain and control can, as elsewhere, provoke ingenious assertions of individuality.

Syllabic-Stress Meter evolved during the Renaissance, as renewed interest in classical literature led poets and critics to adapt Greek and Latin models (whose names are still applied to English verse forms) by simply substituting stresses in English for long syllables in the ancient languages. If we consider the differences between those languages' elements, it's surprising that this yielded a system which worked at all, much less served well for so many centuries. Classical Greek poetry, for instance, builds tensions between two rhythmic elements, both actually heard: the constant lengths of metrical feet and the less regular pitch accents. In English, the vital opposition lies between the anticipated movement of the meter, which may actually be heard only intermittently, and the produced sound of the actual poem. Hopkins terms this contention "counterpoint," although "syncopation" would be more accurate.

In this prosody, the essential form is the five-foot, iambic pentameter line. Though shorter forms have obviously produced many fine poems, they often incline toward a more pronounced formality or toward the easy music of Stress Verse. The five-foot line, accessing both freer and more deeply ingrained qualities, is more conducive to serious portrayal and/or introspection and so has consistently been chosen for our most powerful work.

From time to time, the basic line—ten syllables, stressed on the even-numbered ones—may openly announce itself, as in this very regular line from Shakespeare's Sonnet XXIX:

That **then** I **scorn** to **change** my **state** with **kings**.

In discussing Stress Verse, we noted that stressed syllables chiefly deliver information or opinions about the world, while light syllables most notably carry syntactic instructions. Here, once again, stresses, falling on the main nouns and verbs, specify the central actors and action:

. . . **then** . . . **scorn** . . . **change** . . . **state** . . . **kings**.

though, once again, lacking the function syllables, we might easily misconstrue the sentence. In creating regular iambic verse, then, we order a steady alternation of semantic current:

Function, **CONTENT**, function, **CONTENT**, function,
CONTENT . . . etc.

or, to mimic the sound of the actual line,

Form, **FACT**, form, **FACT**, form, **FACT** . . . etc.

Simultaneously, this alternating flow of semantic current coin-
cides with the passage's rhythmic sound. We earlier noted that
English stressed syllables are, *on the average*, twice as long as
unstressed ones. As a result, iambic, a two-syllable meter, yields a
triple rhythm: such "regular" lines tend to project a rhythm much
like the isochronic beat of a 3/8 musical rhythm

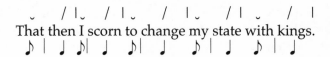

That then I scorn to change my state with kings.

(One need not be concerned that bar marks here do not coincide
with the foot lines. Neither exists as sounds we hear, but merely as
different methods of keeping records. What matters is that stresses
and musical beats, which we do hear, fall together; we scan this
point of attack as the end of iambs or anapests, but notate it as the
start of musical measures.) This rhythm is normative, felt as an
underlying rhythmic ground not only in such regular lines but
inherent beneath its variants. Further, readers come, more by intu-
ition than by conscious attention, to associate iambic forms with just
such a rhythmic impulse.

This rhythm, however, need not rise relentlessly to the surface as
Sidney Lanier and many "time-stress" critics seem to imply. The simple
fact (more truly, the *complicating* fact) is that poetic excellence is seldom,
even in Shakespeare's early work, so strictly regimented. A poem with
much intellectual or emotional range—that is, with much relation to
this world—will necessarily overlay such a model with ebbing and
surging variations and syncopations. We might say that a poem's
actual sound relates to its metrical forms much as the facts of the world
and ourselves relate to Platonic ideals or to social conventions.

Even when stress patterns are regular and musically isochronic, such elements as pauses, polysyllables, consonant clusters and differences of pronunciation or interpretation offer flexibility. Syllables, moreover, do not conform to the strict arithmetical lengths of our musical notation: sixteenth, eighth, quarter, half and whole notes. Our poetic rhythms may thus be less regular, perhaps resembling those of Gregorian chant or of non-Western musics; again, they may resemble those modern musics where the "beat," though present or at least suggested, is less predictable. Igor Stravinsky's "L'Histoire du Soldat" ends with a "Triumphal March for the Devil" where the first nineteen measures show eighteen changes of time signature: bars are marked: 4/4, 5/8, 5/4, 3/4, 2/4, 2/8, 6/8, 7/8 and 3/16. Yet listeners, perhaps sensing the irregularities befitting a drunken celebration, know they're hearing a march.

Similarly, over the length of iambic poems, the sustaining movement will be the 3/8 shown. As we obstruct or alter this pulse of "music" and meaning with prosodic variations—changes from the steady alternation of stress with nonstress—new ranges of emotion and meaning arise. Karl Shapiro and Robert Beum write, in *A Prosody Handbook*:

> A line containing several strong beats will ordinarily seem more vigorous, more packed with energy and meaning.... In English ... intensity of expression is nearly always accompanied by an *abundance of stresses*. Now, in English prose the ratio of nonstresses to stresses ranges from about 2:1 to 3:1.... [I]n the more intense language of poetry, one should expect the ratio to be closer to 1:1, and we find that in fact 9:7 is a common figure.

To this significant observation I would only suggest that the ratio (1:1 or 9:7) given for "poetry" probably holds true only for iambic or trochaic verse. For triple metres or most Stress Verse—where more light syllables intervene between stresses—the ratio should be nearer that of prose (2:1 or 3:1). "Abundance of stresses," then, not merely accompanies but embodies intensity.

Insistent or excited voices, as we've noted, often assume a regular or isochronic "beat"—stresses tend to disperse themselves equidistant in time. Derek Attridge remarks that in such cases, all the stresses in a line or passage approach equal importance, thus highlighting the whole sentence or utterance rather than any hierarchy of significance among its parts. If stresses are less uniformly distributed, on the other hand, local segments of meaning are likely to become more forceful, gaining intensity within the larger construct. Uniform disposition of stresses, then, tends toward the emotional and musical, involving us, rather like dance music, in a kind of unquestioning participation. When emphases are either clustered or dispersed, gradations of meaning are created, so provoking more intellection, more discrimination, more personal dramatic sense.

Variations from the established norm of alternation—particularly spondees, pyrrhics and inverted feet—produce clusters of stress, of meaning and emotion, which are separated by loops of lighter syntactic syllables. Highlighted by their announcement as syncopations or rhythmic variations, these bunchings and slackenings create a voice more personal and immediate, more exacting of attention. These varying intensities of meaning and of music probably coexist as aspects of the same phenomenon: both the rhythm of speech and its emotional coloring appear to be handled in the same part of the brain—an area of the right hemisphere just opposite to Wernicke's area in the left.

The opening of Robert Frost's "Desert Places" bespeaks great emotional turbulence:

> Snow falling and night falling, fast oh fast
> In a field I looked into going past
> And the ground almost covered smooth in snow,
> But a few weeds and stubble showing last.

The poem is obviously in iambic pentameter, yet the first line has a spondee, a pyrrhic, another spondee, the only actual iamb, and perhaps a limping spondee:

/ /|˘ ˘ | / /|˘ / | \ /
Snow falling and night falling, fast oh fast

Some would quarrel with this scansion, saying, for instance, that in the first line, "Snow" has slightly more stress than "fall," so yielding a trochee, while "and" has slightly more than "-ing" thus giving an iamb. Whether true or not, this matter is important only if meter counts more than rhythm, feet more than units of meaning. However, poets do not write—and we do not speak—feet, but rather phrases, lines, sentences. In Frost's line, what strikes the ear is not the steady pulse of iambics but a more urgent and climactic motion: what we measure as the first foot contains two syllables louder and longer than usual; the second foot has two syllables lighter and swifter than usual; then the third has again two stronger syllables. The slower, more emphatic gestures of the first and third feet are further heightened by the interposition of the swift, weak syllables between them. These changes in rhythmic intensity sharply alter the message conveyed.

Frost could easily have regularized this stanza:

The snow was falling; night was falling fast
Across a field I looked at going past;
The ground was almost covered smooth in snow
Though scattered weeds and stems were showing last.

and some might claim that the same information was delivered. Wrong: only a part of that meaning is present, and it is *not* delivered. The sense of urgency, even emergency, has vanished. The fuller revelation of a speaker's mind—not merely of factual perceptions but of feelings and personal qualities—is a poem's concern; we do not go there for a weather report.

This is not to suggest that the poet forces his or her interpretation on readers: the poem *makes available* such discoveries. A crucial measure of any work of art is its range of interpretation—that is, in the amount of inspection it will repay. Readers, like actors, must depend on their own sensitivity to unfold subtexts of character and emotion. For interpreters, as for artists, such matters are often most truly conveyed by manner, by technique. Carl Dennis writes, "To my mind, we are made to feel the speaker's engagement primarily through rhythm." To my mind, that does not overstate the case.

In seeking that variety which can depict individual character-istics, Syllabic-Stress Meter lets us alter either the number of syllables or the number and position of stresses. If we change the syllable count, we are, in effect, writing Stress Verse—and we may be disapproved by classically-oriented critics. We might, for in-stance, add a syllable to the first foot of the line from Shakespeare's sonnet:

> ˘ ˘ / |˘ / | . . . *etc.*
> *So that then* I scorn to change my state with kings.
> ⅜ ♪ ♪ | ♩ ♪| ♩ . . . *etc.*

We could as easily add it to the second foot:

> ˘ / |˘ ˘ / |˘ / | . . . .
> That then **I would scorn** to change my state with kings.
> ⅜ ♪| ♪♪ ♪ | ♩ ♪| . . . .

Indeed, we could add a syllable to each foot, producing a line which, if it stood alone, we might call anapestic. Despite probable small variations, that line would sound roughly as

> ˘ ˘ / |˘ ˘ / |˘ ˘ / | ˘ ˘ / | ˘ ˘ / |
> So that then I would scorn to exchange my estate with a king.
> ♪ ♪| ♪♪ ♪ | ♪ ♪♪♪ ♪ ♪|♪ ♪ ♪|♪

Although we've changed every single foot and measure, no real conflict, strain or syncopation alleviates that underlying and, by now, overbearing 3/8 "beat." This may justify the aforementioned critics: we've taken a liberty but have not contributed to—have actually diminished—the structure of tensions and releases. We have neither brought stresses together, so slowing and emphasizing them, nor separated them widely enough to gain force from their eventual onset. We have, in effect, increased the speed of a dance, decreasing the time for the crucial semantic syllables "scorn" and "-change" to register their pride and exultation. Just such squeezing together of syllables, thus leveling their significance, will concern us again later.

Just as we found in Stress Verse, changing the number or position of stresses offers, to our Western-trained ears, the most significant variants in this 3/8 rhythm. In the following examples, I will offer musical notation to visualize the probable variations in movement, the syncopations that disrupt the expected current of movement—most often replacing the triple movement of the 3/8 time with either two or four notes.

At any point in the line we might add a stress, giving a spondee—as in the fourth foot:

                    . . . | ◡   / | /   / | ◡   / |
That then I'd scorn to change *love's state* with kings.
         . . . . | ♩ ♪| ♩ ₂ ♩ | ♩ ♪ | ♩

or, though less common, in the second foot:

        ◡   / | /   / | ◡   / | . . . .
My true *heart scorns* to change its state with kings.
♪| ♩ ₂ ♩ | ♩   ♪| . . . .

In each case the measure tends to remain constant while two notes (which could equally well be shown in this notation as ♪.♪.) fill the time formerly taken by three eighth notes. As already suggested, however, in less markedly rhythmic passages this might vary; e.g., the length of the quarter note might stay constant while the measure would expand slightly, perhaps opening out to a measure of 2/4. But we would still have a crucial syncopation—two equal notes replacing the expected treble count.

Stresses equally well may fail (except in the last foot where this might undefine the line), replacing an iamb with a pyrrhic foot. It has often been noted that many iambic pentameter lines have only four, instead of five, full stresses, giving us, in effect, four rhythmical units:

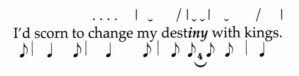

.... | ⌣ / | ⌣ ⌣| ⌣ / |
I'd scorn to change my des*tiny* with kings.
♪| ♩ ♪| ♩ ♪| ♪ ♪₄♪ ♪ | ♩

or:

.... | ⌣ / | ⌣ ⌣| ⌣ / | ....
I'd scorn exchang*ing* *of* my state with kings.
♪| ♩ ♪| ♪ ♪₄♪ ♪ | ♩ ♪| ♩

In the measures notated, four counts fill the time taken earlier by three. This occurs twice in this line by Samuel Daniel:

\   / | ⌣ ⌣| ⌣/| ⌣ ⌣|⌣ / |
Paint shadows in imaginary lines

The theorists mentioned earlier might claim that the second and fourth feet should be scanned as iambs because their second syllables may be slightly stronger than the first. My interest, however, is not in displaying meter as such, but in displaying the rhythms meter can provoke—an element, as we've seen, deeply involved with meaning. And, indeed, we decrease the meaning if we impose, as school children would, the thumping music of "conventional" stresses:

Paint **SHAD**ows **IN** i-**MAG**-i-**NAR**-y **LINES**

so dissolving Daniel's graceful syncopation in favor of a dulling regularity. In his line, the meter with its five measures of 3/8 rhythm, is over-ridden by three units of 2/4 rhythm—two of which have the same effect as paeons ("shadows in imaginary") though here their speed, unlike the awkwardness of our earlier examples from Poe or McGonagall, proves to be an elegance.

Paint shadows in i-mag-i-nar-y lines
♩ | ♪ ♪₄ ♪ ♪| ♪ ♪₄♪ ♪| ♩

The same variation proves equally effective, though with notably less grace, in Yeats'

Mere anarchy is loosed upon the world.

Though such a variation in an iambic poem again rouses attention and increases emotional effect, the tone of that effect is dependent on the qualities and attitudes of the poem's speaker.

Again, excepting for the end of lines, we may invert any foot, replacing an iamb with a trochee. This is most common at the line's beginning, though (especially if the previous line was end-stopped) that may yield only a slight variation:

/   ◡ |◡ / |◡ / |....
Then would I scorn to change my state with kings.
| ♪   ♪ ♪| ♩   ♪|....

Elsewhere in the line, however, such an inversion once again brings stresses to collide, producing a marked syncopation, as here in the third foot:

....|◡   / | / ◡ |◡   / |....
That then I'd scorn *changing* my state with kings.
♪ | ♩ ♪| ♩   ♪|♪♪ ♪| ♩   ♪ | ♩

Once more, we have replaced the basic 3/8 with units of two counts; if we invert the fourth foot

....|◡   / | / ◡ |◡   / |
That then I'd scorn to change *states with* a king.
....| ♩ ♪| ♩   ♪|♪ ♪ ♪| ♩

the stresses and the lighter syllables again bunch themselves separately, yielding a momentary syncopation.

As already suggested, variations are rare at the end of a line but more common and more complex at the beginning. We often find a spondee and a pyrrhic foot combined, in either order. Should the spondee come first, then the light syllables of the pyrrhic foot give us again what is in effect a paeon, giving the same four-note syncopation noted earlier:

/ / | ⌣ ⌣| ⌣ / | | . . . .

Scorn rises in the heart to change my state with kings.

Should the pyrrhic come first, this often gives a movement whose notation is more complicated:

⌣ ⌣ | / / | | . . . .

That the heart scorns to change its state with kings.

It is also common in iambic lines to drop the light first syllable, giving a nine-syllable "truncated" line with an accent at both beginning and end, though occasionally the first stress may fail. Further, at the end of such truncated lines, one may add an extra light syllable, giving a "feminine" ending, but since that moves us from iambic to trochaic forms, this should be considered separately.

* * * * * * * *

Since the so-called falling meters—trochaic and truncated lines—have the same basic alteration of stressed and light syllables, we might expect them to share the same underlying 3/8 rhythm we've noted in iambics, except that, because we lose the light syllable which begins the line, we would drop the corresponding pickup note of the rhythm. At times, falling meters do produce such a rhythm. The young John Milton wrote a graceful song which deftly mixes iambic, trochaic and truncated meters with both pentameter and tetrameter lines:

SONG ON A MAY MORNING

Now the bright morning Star, Day's harbinger,
Comes dancing from the East, and leads with her
The Flow'ry May, who from her green lap throws
The yellow cowslip and the pale primrose.
    Hail, bounteous May that does inspire
    Mirth and youth and warm desire!
    Woods and groves are of thy dressing,
    Hill and Dale doth boast thy blessing.
Thus we salute thee with our early Song,
And welcome thee and wish thee long.

A great deal of skill has gone into blending the heavier, stress-loaded iambic pentameter of the first quatrain into the lighter and swifter tetrameters of the second. Though line 5 is still iambic, it has been shortened to tetrameter, the typical length of falling meters—which we do find in lines 6, 7, and 8. Again, the metrical shift is alleviated by the ambiguous masculine or feminine rhyme "inspire/desire" and by the later tendency to link light syllables to following stressed syllables ("and youth . . . and warm . . . desire," etc.) helps maintain the iambic rhythms of the opening stanza throughout the central section. Thus, most readers, while conscious of the difference in movement, will be less than aware of the metrical changes.

But this is the exception. Falling meters usually produce a very different movement from the iambic triple rhythm, strongly inclining toward a duple rhythm. This will be heard in most people's reading of "The Tyger":

Tyger, tyger, burning bright
In the forest of the night,

or again in the wedding benediction from *The Tempest*:

Honour, riches, marriage-blessing,
Long continuance, and increasing,

Such examples often include many disyllabic words (or linked pairs of monosyllables) where the accent falls on the first, so embodying a trochee ("Tyger . . . burning . . . forest," and "Honour, riches, marriage-blessing"). As Attridge points out in *The Rhythms of English Poetry*, in such cases stress may no longer coincide with length—though the first syllable keeps its stress, the second may gain length or be followed by a pause. At times we hear something like the "snap rhythms" of Hungarian and Scottish folk songs; more often, though, the syllables approximate equal lengths and present a rather sturdy 2/4. Within that movement, however, the frequent failing of stresses often yields a paeonic movement of four short syllables, quickening and livening the duple rhythm.

Unlike the change we found in Milton's song, the following poem by Philip Larkin establishes a trochaic meter, shifting to iambics at its climax, then returning to the falling rhythm. Again, most readers will feel this change sharply but may well attribute this to the solemnity of subject, unaware that, at least in part, this tone is produced by the rhythmic conversion.

THE EXPLOSION

On the day of the explosion
Shadows pointed toward the pithead:
In the sun the slagheap slept.

Down the lane came men in pitboots
Coughing oath-edged talk and pipe-smoke,
Shouldering off the freshened silence.

One chased after rabbits, lost them;
Came back with a nest of lark's eggs;
Showed them; lodged them in the grasses.

So they passed in beards and moleskins,
Fathers, brothers, nicknames, laughter,
Through the tall gates standing open.

At noon, there came a tremor; cows
Stopped chewing for a second; sun,
Scarfed as in a heat-daze, dimmed.

The dead go on before us, they
Are sitting in God's house in comfort,
We shall see them face to face—

Plain as lettering in the chapels
It was said, and for a second
Wives saw men of the explosion

Larger than in life they managed—
Gold as on a coin, or walking
Somehow from the sun towards them,

One showing the eggs unbroken.

After four stanzas of falling meters, quickened and colloquialized by failed initial stresses, we shift at the moment of the explosion to iambics. At first disguised by run-on lines, "cows / Stopped chewing . . . ; sun / Scarfed as in a heat daze . . . ," the broader iambic 3/8 is fully revealed in the funeral eulogy: "*The dead go on before us . . .*" We then fall back to steady trochaics in the ending's recollection of the men whose passage we've associated with that rhythm.

Such interferences of contrasting movement may occur not only between longer passages or groups of stanzas, but on a smaller scale, from line to line. W. H. Auden provides an example:

THE FALL OF ROME

The piers are pummelled by the waves;
In a lonely field the rain
Lashes an abandoned train;
Outlaws fill the mountain caves.

219

Fantastic grow the evening gowns;
Agents of the Fisc pursue
Absconding tax-defaulters through
The sewers of provincial towns.

In these first stanzas, lines may be either iambic or truncated. Continued through three more stanzas of details (drawn as often from our decadence as from Rome's), the surprising leaps of subject matter, period and scene are accented by shifts in rhythmic movement, especially by the assertive onset of the initial stress in truncated lines. These variances between contrasting lines or pairs of lines are broadened as the poem turns from the human to the natural world; aided by the easy flow of initial and final trochaic lines, the period of rhythmic movement expands from the line to the stanza:

Unendowed with wealth or pity,
Little birds with scarlet legs,
Sitting on their speckled eggs,
Eye each flu-infected city.

The light pace of these falling rhythms is then carried on into the astonishing final stanza, which depicts the unimpeded rush of nature beyond human bounds:

Altogether elsewhere, vast
Herds of reindeer move across
Miles and miles of golden moss,
Silently and very fast.

That speed is embodied in the falling meter and the use of enjambment across line breaks. The passage could easily be rewritten in the iambics heard earlier:

While elsewhere, thundering and vast,
Migrating herds of reindeer cross
Unbroken miles of golden moss
In silence and exceeding fast.

so losing the headlong surge of unadulterated nature. Enjambments no longer defeat our expectations; final stresses no longer burst across line breaks to collide with the initial stress of the next line. Without that impetuous movement, the magic is lost.

Even more characteristic than such examples of rhythmic interference and conflict on larger levels is the constant small-scale competition (often occurring within the line) of rhythms inherent to falling meters. We may cite one of Auden's most famous lyrics:

> Lay your sleeping head, my love,
> Human on my faithless arm;
> Time and fevers burn away
> Individual beauty from
> Thoughtful children, and the grave
> Proves the child ephemeral:
> But in my arms till break of day
> Let the living creature lie,
> Mortal, guilty, but to me
> The entirely beautiful.
>
> Soul and body have no bounds:
> To lovers as they lie upon
> Her tolerant enchanted slope
> In their ordinary swoon,
> Grave the vision Venus sends
> Of supernatural sympathy,
> Universal love and hope;
> While an abstract insight wakes
> Among the glaciers and the rocks
> The hermit's sensual ecstasy.
>
> Certainty, fidelity
> On the stroke of midnight pass
> Like vibrations of a bell,
> And fashionable madmen raise
> Their pedantic boring cry:
> Every farthing of the cost,

All the dreaded cards foretell
Shall be paid, but from this night
Not a whisper, not a thought,
Not a kiss nor look be lost.

Beauty, midnight, vision dies:
Let the winds of dawn that blow
Softly round your dreaming head
Such a day of sweetness show
Eye and knocking heart may bless,
Find the mortal world enough;
Noons of dryness see you fed
By the involuntary powers,
Nights of insult let you pass
Watched by every human love.

The first line establishes a basic pattern most easily scanned as a truncated line of four stresses, one at the beginning and one at the end. While seven of these forty lines might be scanned as iambic and, unlike "The Fall of Rome," there are no actual trochaic lines, many factors do incline toward the duple rhythm we associate with it: most lines begin with a stress; further, we find the familiar prevalence of disyllabic words or pairs of words stressed on the first syllable, ("sleeping, human, faithless," etc.). Moreover, at least eighteen failed stresses contribute to this rhythm, though six of those are at line ends, helping counter the tendency to end-stop and giving more fluidity than truncated lines usually have.

On the other hand, besides those lines with an added light first syllable, we also find numerous examples of local iambic movement ("my love ... away ... the grave ... of day ... entirely beautiful"). Thus, we experience a constant, unresolved conflict between an iambic 3/8 and a trochaic 2/4 rhythm. To my ear, that tension helps body forth the poem's combination and conflict of romantic and philosophical passions. Such continuous and unresolved small-scale tensions between opposing rhythmic impulses seem typical of the falling meters, in contrast to iambics' tendency to project one basic and underlying rhythm which, on a larger scale, is contrasted with strongly marked variations.

Finally, I should note that such conflicts of rhythm may be caused as much by the way the mind orders and registers what it hears as by the way we produce speech: our clocks say *tik, tik, tik;* we hear *tik-TOK, tik-TOK, tik-TOK.* Robert Gjerdingen of the Music Department of SUNY Stony Brook has reported on experiments in which certain acoustic signals were perceived by professional and student musicians as triple rhythms, yet when the same signals were played backwards, most heard those sounds as "a slightly jazzy example of 2/4 time." That perception curiously parallels the rhythmic switch we found when reversing iambics into trochaic or truncated lines. Although Attridge has contributed important insights in these areas, I must agree with his suggestion that more research could yield significant insights for critics and for poets as well.

*   *   *   *   *   *   *   *

I have delayed discussing the triple meters—anapests and dactyls—because they are less common and less often successful in English. Earlier we noted that one may question whether to consider truncated lines as iambic or trochaic; similarly, in the triple meters, the freedom to add or drop light syllables at the beginning and ending of lines may lead one to question whether to label verses as anapestic or dactylic. This, however, is only a question of the handiest method of bookkeeping; we do not hear the rhythmic difference between anapests and dactyls which we've noted between iambics and trochaics. Encountering such a splendid poem as Thomas Hardy's "No Buyers"—obviously in triple meter—it little matters whether one scans it as anapests, dactyls or Stress Verse. In each case, we have the same number of main stresses and the preference for separating them with two weaker syllables. The real issue must involve how Hardy turns verses we might expect to be light and buoyant toward the seriousness befitting an image of destitution in old age. My concern here will be with the rhythms rising from these triple meters, their emotional effect, and why they have so often proved problematic.

It may seem surprising that these triple meters, whose final effect differs so sharply from that of iambics, also tend to yield a

3/8 rhythm. That was remarked upon earlier when we turned the last line of Shakespeare's Sonnet XXIX into anapests:

> So that then I would scorn to exchange my estate with a
>   king.

One would find much the same rhythm in these shorter lines of Byron:

> The Assyrian came down like a wolf on the fold
> And his cohorts were gleaming in silver and gold

Or in Swinburne, Lanier or, as here, Poe:

> The skies they were ashen and sober;
>   The leaves they were crispèd and sere—
>   The leaves they were withering and sere:
> It was night, in the lonesome October
>   Of my most immemorial year:
> It was hard by the dim lake of Auber
>   In the misty mid region of Weir—
>   It was down by the dank tarn of Auber
> In the ghoul-haunted woodland of Weir.

The movement is insistently isochronic: main stresses are unvaryingly equidistant, never colliding, failing or fluctuating. Moreover, despite a few small variations, the rhythmic sense is that all syllables, stressed or not, are equal in length. The basic pattern within the 3/8 will be |♪♪♪| rather than the |♩♪| of iambics.

It was night, in the lonesome October

♪ ♪ | ♪ , ♪ ♪ | ♪ ♪ ♪ | ♪ ♪ ♪ 𝄾𝄾

Of my most immemorial year:

♪ ♪ | ♪ ♪ ♪ | ♪ ♪ ♪ | ♩ 𝄾𝄽

(This notation treats the only real variation, "withering," as three full syllables, though most readers would contract it to "with'ring," returning the rhythm to the basic pattern.) Though later stanzas offer a few secondary stresses, the relentless 3/8 has already numbed one's responses.

Let me recall Shapiro and Beum's statement, "In English . . . intensity of expression is nearly always accompanied by an *abundance of stresses*." Here, the ratio of light to stressed syllables which they suggest, nearly 1:1, has risen to 2:1. The stressed syllables, scarcely longer than function syllables, do not command the time for recognition of their richer meaning and emotional content. An unfortunate side effect is that, as the verse rushes through these oncharging syllables, many poets (since stresses will not receive full salience, full significance) are more likely to admit trite or expectable filler.

As a result, triple meters are most often used for light verse and musical pieces. (Paeonics, where the ratio will rise to 3:1, are unsuitable as a continued form for anything much weightier than patter songs.) "My Thing Is My Own" is a typical salacious eighteenth-century theater song (set to the tune of "Lilliburlero") in which a young woman cites the various gallants interested in her "thing." The verses, amusing but not particularly memorable, scan most easily as anapests:

> I, a tender young maid, have been courted by many,
> Of all sorts and trades as ever was any;
> A spruce haberdasher first spake to me fair,
> But I would have nothing to do with small ware.
> > My thing is my own and I'll keep it so still,
> > Yet other young lasses may do what they will.

In most stanzas, the stresses (whether sung or spoken) remain equidistant with a fairly constant pair of light syllables between and only occasional secondary stresses, as above in "tender young maid." Yet, in the seventh stanza something surprising happens: the rhythm of the spoken verse varies from the expectations of the meter and the "beat" of the music:

˘ / |˘ \ ˘ | ˘ / / | ˘ ˘ / |
A gentleman that did talk much of his Grounds,
˘ / |˘ ˘ /|˘ / ˘ |˘ / / |
His Horses, his Setting Dogs and his Grey-Hounds.

The syllable count is unvaried, but in the first line a light secondary stress has shifted back from the fifth to the fourth syllable (from "that" to "-man"); in the next line it has shifted from the eighth to the seventh (from "and" to "Dogs"). Further, each line has what, in iambics, we would scan as a pyrrhic followed by a spondee ("that did talk much" and "and his Grey-Hounds"). Thus, these lines as spoken break the monotonous pattern, giving both dips of lighter syllables and peaks of joined stresses—a variant which hovers above the underlying pulse much like the syncopations we found in iambic verse.

The musical setting, however, tends to enforce that regular beat and meter, so prompting the singer to give conventional, unmeaning stress and duration to inconsequential words: "**that** did talk" or "**and** his Grey-Hounds." This explains why song-writers usually avoid the stress variations which, in poems, provide more meaningful gesture but, in songs, demand skills that singers in English seldom command. If this seems to justify the claim that "the more music, the less meaning," I would argue that the rhythms in this text, as spoken, are more meaningful, more truly musical than are the thumping regularities of our musical practices. The Western tradition of simplified musical rhythms has proven fertile for the evolution of harmony, counterpoint, melodic development and orchestration, but such effects are unavailable to speech or poetry. The question is not merely what we mean by "meaning," but what we mean by "music."

Even in light and comic verse, more satisfying rhythms are often found by varying the number and position of stresses. Ralph Hodgson's "Eve" sets up a line of dactylic dimeter:

Eve, with her basket, was
Deep in the bells and grass,
Wading in bells and grass
Up to her knees,
Picking a dish of sweet
Berries and plums to eat,
Down in the bells and grass
Under the trees.

Mute as a mouse in a
Corner the cobra lay,
Curled round a bough of the
Cinnamon tall. . . .
Now to get even and
Humble proud heaven and
Now was the moment or
Never at all.

"Eva!" Each syllable
Light as a flower fell, . . .

Enjambed and runover lines, slant rhymes which can vary from one
to three syllables ("even and / . . . heaven and"), rhymes that fall on
normally unstressed syllables, risqué rhymes which are suggested
but never appear ("bells and grass / Up to her knees")—enliven the
basic pulse. Keeping the syllable count, Hodgson adds stresses
("Curled round a" or "Humble proud heaven"). This happens most
often in a line's second half, replacing the usual dactyl ($/˘˘$) with a
foot ($/˘/$), much like the Greek and Latin amphimacer ($-˘-$), and
yielding a movement in which we may question whether a line has
two or three stresses.

Oh, had our simple Eve
Seen through the make-believe

Such stress loading is most marked at the climax, where the serpent's
whisper is echoed and mocked by the roistering of the damned:

Picture her crying
Outside in the lane,
Eve, with no dish of sweet
Berries and plums to eat,
Haunting the gate of the
Orchard in vain . . .
Picture the lewd delight
Under the hill tonight —
"Eva!" the toast goes round,
"Eva!" again.

This ultimate salute is prepared by a foot of three nearly equal stresses ("toast goes round"), slowing and heightening that bawdy shout of celebration.

We find similar stress variations in a poem of William Blake's, one of our finest examples of triple meter:

AH, SUNFLOWER

Ah, Sun-flower! weary of time,
That countest the steps of the Sun
Seeking after that sweet golden clime
Where the traveller's journey is done

Where the Youth pined away with desire,
And the pale Virgin, shrouded in snow
Arise from their graves, and aspire
Where my Sun-flower wishes to go.

The first line is heavily stress-loaded—

\ | / \ ⌣ | / ⌣ ⌣| /
Ah, Sun-flower, weary of time

then balanced by the prototypic second. Again, the third line is slowed and emphasized by added stresses:

\ ˘ | / ˘ ˘ ˘ | / \ ˘ | /
Seeking after that sweet, golden clime

and returns to regularity in the fourth. Both fifth and sixth lines have added weights, but the seventh, dropping its first syllable, takes surprising buoyance from the word "Arise." Adding the omitted syllable, "Will arise . . . ," or "Can arise . . ." will prove the sensitivity of Blake's ear.

Triple meters, though conducive to such light and lyric motion in extended poems, can, if used intermittently, convey bursts of passion, as we heard when these currents swept into Tennyson's "Break, Break, Break":

> O well for the fisherman's boy
>   That he shouts with his sister at play!
> O well for the sailor lad,
>   That he sings in his boat on the bay!

In more extended use, these meters can convey an emotional involvement close to enchantment, as in Hardy's "The Voice":

> Woman much missed, how you call to me, call to me,
> Saying that now you are not as you were
> When you had changed from the one who was all to me,
> But as at first, when our day was fair.

The poem's ending is remarkably canny; after three such dactylic stanzas, the speaker, resorting to duple meters, pulls himself up from his hallucination, only to have the earlier rhythms surface again, heralding the return of the dead wife's voice:

> Thus I; faltering forward,
>   Leaves around me falling,
> Wind oozing thin through the thorn from norward,
>   And the woman calling.

For a final example, I will turn to another poem about a haunting and beloved voice, a poem I have previously cited in other contexts:

PIANO

—D. H. Lawrence

Softly, in the dusk, a woman is singing to me
Taking me back down the vista of years, till I see
A child sitting under the piano, in the boom of the
    tingling strings
And pressing the small, poised feet of a mother who
    smiles as she sings.
In spite of myself, the insidious mastery of song
Betrays me back, till the heart of me weeps to belong
To the old Sunday evenings at home, with winter outside
And hymns in the cozy parlor, the tinkling piano our guide.

So now it is vain for the singer to burst into clamor
With the great black piano appassionato. The glamour
Of childish days is upon me, my manhood is cast
Down in the flood of remembrance, I weep like a child for
    the past.

As in the song by Milton, we have a blend of pentameter and hexameter lines. Reining in any urge toward a gallop, Lawrence employs not only conflict between line lengths and syntactic units, as well as stress variations like those we've been discussing, but also a variant I have not encountered elsewhere. Not only may the light syllables between stresses drop from two to one, but in several places, a third nonstress is admitted, giving in effect a paeon:

| / ˘ ˘ ˘ | / ˘ | / ˘ ˘ | / ˘ ˘ | /
Softly, in the dusk, a woman is singing to me.

This happens twice in the third line:

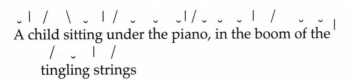

⌣ | / \ ⌣ | / ⌣ ⌣ ⌣| / ⌣ ⌣ ⌣ | / ⌣ ⌣ |
A child sitting under the piano, in the boom of the |
/ ⌣ | /
   tingling strings

(echoing, perhaps, that resonance of the child's experience), then again in the fifth line:

⌣ | / ⌣ ⌣| / ⌣ ⌣| / ⌣ ⌣ | / ⌣ ⌣ ⌣| /
In spite of myself, the insidious mastery of song.

Here, there is a possibility of contracting "mastery" into two syllables. This possibility might suggest that, since open vowels collide in the first and third lines, those might also be counted as elisions (theoretical contractions). We have no idea what Lawrence thought about this; one scarcely imagines him to be prone to such Miltonic casuistries as counting "Softly, in" or "piano, in" as having only two syllables each.

Despite all evidence to the contrary, we still imagine Lawrence as dashing off verses at white heat, nearly improvised. In fact, he probably reworked this poem from 1907 to 1918. He could easily have made these lines more regular:

> Softly, at dusk, a woman is singing to me
> A child underneath the piano, hearing the boom of the
>   strings
> In spite of myself, the insidious power of song

Such changes might involve slight losses of literal content, yet I suspect that the real cause of Lawrence's variants is that the enchantment which the triple meters help depict is more insidious if less insistent. The prosier insertions help anchor us to the real world, where the mother's remembered "glamour" (in the old sense, an evil magic) overcomes the present's appassionato song. Diluting this triple meter—which often saps meaning from crucial words, sweeping us into an almost mindless music—more involves the poem with the factual, so intensifying its meaning.

Further, the loops of light syllables at the end of line five—"the insidious mastery of song"—add force to the crucial run-on "Betrays." Again, the spillover of the penultimate line makes even more dramatic the sexual failure: "my manhood is cast/ Down . . ." Rendering powerfully an erotic impotence, Lawrence employs a verse form usually conspicuous and neglectful of meaning but exercises such skill that most readers are caught up in the content and sound, paying little or no attention to the metrics which played a crucial role in its creation.

*   *   *   *   *   *   *   *

I earlier suggested that the consistent "beat" of isochronic verse might be related to the mother's heartbeat and might approach, in its constancy, a kind of "ideal" (a bit like the child sitting under the piano "in the boom of the tingling strings.") If that seems far-fetched, I will go a step farther and suggest that the less regular rhythms of our more ambitious poems may reflect the brain's effort to resolve this ideal accountability with its own rhythmic nature and its effort to convert into language the varying and ever-shifting facts of an unstable and fractious world.

ACKNOWLEDGMENTS

Grateful acknowledgment is made to the editors of the following journals and publications where these essays, or earlier versions, appeared first: *Shenandoah* and *The Southern Review*. The first section of "Pulse and Impulse" appeared in *Poetspeak*, Paul Janeczko, ed., Bradbury, Scarsdale. An early version of the second section appeared in *Singular Voices*, Stephen Berg, ed., Avon, New York.

W. H. AUDEN: "The Fall of Rome" from *W. H. Auden Collected Poems* by W. H. Auden. Copyright © 1947 by W. H. Auden. Reprinted by Permission of Random House, Inc. "Lullaby," copyright © 1972 by W. H. Auden, from *W. H. Auden: The Collected Poems* by W. H. Auden. Used by permission of Random House.

G. K. CHESTERTON: "Three Ravens" by G. K. Chesterton, reprinted by permission of A. P. Watt, Ltd.

E. E. CUMMINGS: The lines from "anyone lived in a pretty how town." Copyright 1940, © 1968, 1991 by the Trustees for the E. E. Cummings Trust. "l(a". Copyright © 1958, 1986, 1991 by the Trustees for the E. E. Cummings Trust, from *Complete Poems: 1904–1962* by E. E. Cummings, edited by George Firmage. Used by permission of Liveright Publishing Corporation.

MONA VAN DUYN: "What the Motorcycle Said," from *If It Be Not I (Merciful Disguises)*, by Mona Van Duyn, reprinted by permission of Alfred A. Knopf, a Division of Random House, Inc.

T. S. ELIOT: Excerpt from the *Selected Prose of T. S. Eliot*, copyright 1975 by Valerie Eliot, reprinted by permission of Harcourt, Inc.

ROBERT FRANCIS: "Silent Poem," from *Collected Poems: 1936-1976*. Copyright 1976 by Robert Francis. Used by permission of The University of Massachusetts Press, Amherst.

ROBERT FROST: "Desert Places," "Home Burial," "Out, Out," and "Desert Places" from *The Poetry of Robert Frost*, edited by Edward Connery Lathem. Copyright 1928, © 1969 by Henry Holt & Co., copyright 1936, 1956 by Robert Frost. Reprinted by permission of Henry Holt & Co., LLC.

ALLEN GINSBERG: All lines from "A Supermarket in California" from *Collected Poems 1947-1980* by Allen Ginsberg, copyright © 1955 by Allen Ginsberg. Reprinted by permission of HarperCollins Publishers Inc.

D.H. LAWRENCE: "Piano," by D. H. Lawrence, from *The Complete Poems of D. H. Lawrence*, edited by V. de Sola Pinto & F. W. Roberts, copyright © 1964, 1971 by Angelo Ravagli and C. M. Weekley, Executors of the Estate of Frieda Lawrence Ravagli. Used by permission of Viking Penguin, a division of Penguin Putnam, Inc.

PHILIP LARKIN: "The Explosion" from *Collected Poems* by Philip Larkin. Copyright © 1988, 1989 bt the Estate of Philip Larkin. Reprinted by permission of Farrar, Straus and Giroux, LLC.

MARIANNE MOORE, "The Fish" (excerpt) and "The Monkeys" (excerpt). Reprinted with the permission of Scribner, a Division of Simon & Schuster from *The Collected Poems of Marianne Moore*. Copyright 1935 by Marianne Moore; copyright renewed © 1963 by Marianne Moore and T. S. Eliot. "Spencer's Ireland" (excerpt) and "A Carriage from Sweden" (excerpt). Reprinted with the permission of Scribner, a Division of Simon & Schuster from *The Collected Poems of Marianne Moore*. Copyright 1941, 1944 by Marianne Moore; copyright renewed © 1969, 1972 by Marianne Moore.

OCTAVIO PAZ: Excerpt from "Reading and Contemplation" in *Convergences, Essays on Art and Literature* by Octavio Paz, copyright © 1973 by Editorial Joaquín Mortiz, S. A., copyright © 1984, 1983, 1979, by Editorial Seix Barral, S. A., copyright © 1983, 1983, 1979 by Octavio Paz, English translation by Helen Lange copyright © 1987 by Harcourt Inc. reprinted by permission of Harcourt, Inc.

EDWIN ARLINGTON ROBINSON: "Mr. Flood's Party." Reprinted with the permission of Scribner, a Division of Simon & Schuster from *The Collected Poems of Edwin Arlington Robinson*. Copyright 1935 by MacMillan Publishing Company; copyright renewed © 1963 by Ruth Nivison and Barbara R. Holt.

WILLIAM CARLOS WILLIAMS: "Asphodel, That Greeny Flower" (excerpt) and "Spring and All, Section I" (excerpt), by William Carlos Williams, from *Collected Poems: 1909-1939*, Volume I, copyright © 1938 by New Directions Publishing Corp. Reprinted by permission of New Directions Publishing Corp.

ABOUT THE AUTHOR

Responsible for the emergence of American confessional poetry, W. D. Snodgrass won the 1960 Pulitzer Prize for Poetry for his first book, *Heart's Needle*. He saw much of our domestic suffering as occurring against a backdrop of a more universal suffering inherent in the whole of human experience. Snodgrass followed that astonishing work with *After-Experience; The Führer Bunker: A Cycle of Poems in Progress* (BOA Editions, Ltd., 1977), nominated for the National Book Award and produced for the American Place Theater; *Each in His Season* (BOA, 1993); *The Fuehrer Bunker: The Complete Cycle* (BOA, 1995); and *Selected Translations* (BOA, 1998). His *After-Images: Autobiographical Sketches* (BOA) was published in 1999. His critical study, *De/Compositions: 101 Good Poems Gone Wrong* (Graywolf Press, 2001), was a finalist for the National Book Critics Circle Award in criticism. He lives with his wife, critic and translator Kathleen Snodgrass, in Erieville, New York, and San Miguel de Allende, Mexico.

INDEX

BOA EDITIONS, LTD.
AMERICAN READER SERIES

COLOPHON

To Sound Like Yourself: Essays on Poetry, by W. D. Snodgrass, was set in Palatino and Sonata fonts with Hoefler Text Ornaments, by Richard Foerster, York Beach, ME. The cover was designed by Lisa Mauro/Mauro Design. Manufacturing was by McNaughton & Gunn, Saline, MI. Cover art, "W. D. and the Amigo" is by DeLoss McGraw.

Special Donations by the following people helped make the publication of this book possible:

Jacquelynn Baas • Michael Broomfield
Nancy & Alan Cameros
Carole Cooper & Howard Haims
Burch Craig • Sybil Craig
Dr. William & Shirley Ann Crosby
Ron & Susan Dow
Dr. Henry & Beverly French
Dane & Judy Gordon
Suzanne & Gerard Gouvernet
Don & Marge Grinols
Deb & Kip Hale • Sandi Henschel
Peter & Robin Hursh
Robert & Willy Hursh
Richard Garth & Mimi Hwang
Dorothy & Henry Hwang
X. J. Kennedy
Suzanne Owens • Boo Poulin
Deborah Ronnen • Dona Rosu
Andrea & Paul Rubery • Jane Schuster
Robert B. Shea • Dr. Loubert Suddaby
Pat & Michael Wilder • Mark Williams